Endorseme.

Unsure how to teach your children morality and responsibility? Mary Lee Dey has written a book filled with wisdom and practical advice that takes you step by step through every aspect of raising happy, holy, and responsible children. Not only will parents who use this book find that their children grow in responsibility and morality but they will also find family members deepening their affection toward one another, which in turn produces peace and harmony in the family. I urge you to read *Speak to Your Children.*

> Mary Ann Budnik, author of the
> ***Raise Happy Children Series***

Speak to Your Children addresses the issues you need to address, but sometimes fear to address, with your children offering useful information and tips from the perspective of an experienced Catholic mother. This is a serious book for serious parents.

> David C. Reardon, Ph.D.
> Director, Elliot Institute
> Author, *Making Abortion Rare*

Speak To Your Children is outstanding and would be a great parenting aid. I am recommending it to all my grandchildren who are now starting their families.

> Josephine Shafer
> Mother, Grandmother, and Great Grandmother

Speak to Your Children

Speak to Your Children

A Handy Catholic Parenting Guide
for Concise, Faith-filled Conversations
with Kids about Discipline, Decision-making,
Truth, and *Life*

Mary Lee Dey

iUniverse, Inc.
New York Lincoln Shanghai

Speak to Your Children
A Handy Catholic Parenting Guide for Concise, Faith-filled Conversations with Kids about Discipline, Decision-making, Truth, and *Life*

iUniverse, Inc.

For information address:
iUniverse, Inc.
2021 Pine Lake Road, Suite 100
Lincoln, NE 68512
www.iuniverse.com

ISBN: 0-595-31922-X

Printed in the United States of America

NIHIL OBSTAT:
Very Reverend John T. Folda
Censor Librorum

IMPRIMATUR:
Most Reverend Fabian W. Bruskewitz
Bishop of Lincoln

March 25, 2004

The NIHIL OBSTAT and IMPRIMATUR are official declarations that a book
or pamphlet is free from doctrinal or moral error. No implication is contained therein
that those who have granted the NIHIL OBSTAT and IMPRIMATUR agree with the
contents, opinions, or statements expressed.

Cover © 2004
Cover illustration by Sarah Vaughn
Chapter illustrations by Mary Lee Dey

This book is hereby dedicated to Jesus, His Blessed Mother, Mary, and Saint Joseph for the preservation of the family.

Acknowledgments

With gratitude to God for parents George and Frances Tvrdy;
children and their spouses Joe, Mary Clare, Jean, Tim,
Jim, Kim, Mike, Kathy; and their families;
and especially husband Darrell

and to God's other angels:
Mary Elizabeth Anderson; Mary and Terri Tvrdy;
Julie and Gary Hatfield; Jeanne Schutte;
Neda Simonds, JoAnne Shafer; Gary Horton;
Vivian Dudro, editorial assistant at Ignatius Press;
Judie Brown, president and Camille Murphy
of American Life League;
Couple to Couple League;
Stephen Koob, editor at One More Soul;
and Father Thomas Kuffel

Glory and praise to the One who makes it happen

Contents

Letter to Parents

Theodore Roethke once wrote, "So much of adolescence is an ill-defined dying, an intolerable waiting, a longing for another place and time, another condition."

Adolescence need not be ill defined and intolerable; it can be a magnificent faith-filled journey. That is the reason I developed this book *Speak to Your Children*. I wanted a succinct way to help parents raise wise, mature children—children who understand life issues—children who can withstand negative pressures that surround them. Young people who learn the truths and skills of this book have an excellent chance of reaching adulthood with faith, integrity, and a respect for life. They will pass these truths on for generations to come.

For many years, I worked with crisis services in schools and pregnancy centers. The children I counseled differed little from the ones you or I might raise, at least in their brightness and naiveté. In every case, however different, the children wanted to talk—to talk about abusive families, sex, drugs, runaways, depression, crime, cults, poverty, and whatever else concerned them. Unfortunately, their outlook on life usually came from the popular idea of the day, no matter how false and damaging it happened to be.

The Church understands that parents are the first teachers of their children's faith and morals. We Catholic parents do not want immoral television shows or movies, deviant groups, courts, or birth control centers to indoctrinate our children. Yet far too often our children's information, rather misinformation, comes from these sources.

All children need guidance from their parents, and most parents are eager to raise knowledgeable, prudent children who can withstand the negative influences around them. I have found, however, that many parents do not know where to begin. Most parents, my husband and I included (we have four adult children and seven grandchildren), need a little help with raising children in our increasingly anti-life and anti-faith culture.

Considering how children learn twelve years of math and English, why can't they learn about God, love, and life (partly via this book) from us for at least as many years? Why can't they learn better than we did? Then they would have a strong foundation for Catholic adulthood, and we parents who had raised them well would be able to say, "I taught them all I could. Now they can make a safe and confident passage into adulthood."

Through not only work in crisis management and as a Catholic Adult Education leader, but also as a certified teacher in Natural Family Planning and as a certified Family Life director, I learned there is much room for hope in spite of our youth's alarming problems. I found many parents eager to teach truth, and many young people open to learning it. This book is for them. Parents may use this book not as a formal treatise on the subjects at hand, but as a tool for opening the doors of conversation with children.

Read, listen, converse, and pray—God works in mysterious ways. To us, the Lamb of God gives peace even in the midst of our troubled world.

Sincerely yours in Christ, Mary Lee Dey

Introduction

"…I laid a foundation, and another man is building upon it…." (1 Corinthians 3:10). This Catholic parents' book shows you how to snatch magic moments of conversation with your children, as Jesus did with us.

This book has seven chapters on life issues. Chapters I, II, and III help you guide children to develop love and respect, practice discipline, and recognize negative influences. These act as a foundation to combat drugs, sexual abuse, depression, and violence discussed in Chapters IV, V, and VI. Lastly, Chapter VII shows you how to teach your children about the I-beams of faith.

This book also helps you as parents do the following:

1. Think through the gradual manner you learned about faith, morals, and life issues, and then decide how to teach these to your children in short sessions.

2. Establish positive communication with your children.

3. Learn firm and loving ways to deal with your children's resistance to your authority.

4. Alert your children to negative peer pressure and show them how they can use the acronym SCARE to resist anti-life and anti-Christian influences.

5. Inform your children about God's loving will for them and about the difference between right and wrong, good and evil, life and death.

6. Add your family's talents to community projects to enlarge your children's hearts for others.

7. Acquire answers for your children's questions regarding the Catholic faith.

Love and faith are the central ideas in this book. Each chapter begins with a note on them. Morality that is taught with love and faith sticks together as glue sticks between fingers. When you run into difficulty, come back to these parts.

For children under 5, you will want to share parts of Exercises 1, 2, 6, and 7 on God's love, so that you, as parents can build a strong family life before you begin having formal conversations with your children. Read for yourself all chapters, especially Exercises 12 to 17 on discipline and 56 on faith and purity. Young children need love, hugs, "time-outs," and forgiveness. Live by good example. Attend Church faithfully and teach them to pray.

For ages 5 to 11, let your kids be kids and concentrate on faith and virtue. Let them have a normal, fun childhood, somewhat free from the burdensome knowledge of how others sin. You, however, may want to discuss some of Chapter I. Implement Exercises 56 and 57, and *carefully* selected parts of 49. Then, explain in your own shining words any Bible verses in other chapters. Even better, acquire a children's Bible and read it aloud often. You might read one passage per night after you have said prayers (at end of book). Children's stories of saints and heroes are also inspiring for this age. Read for yourself especially Exercises 15-20, on discipline; Chapter V introduction on sexuality; and Exercise 70 on faith.

After reviewing Chapter I with ages 11 to 13, examine other chapters and—depending on their maturity, exposure to media, and type of parochial, public, or homeschool—decide what would be appropriate discussion material for them. Be selective. This gives you the opportunity to teach your children at their own level of understanding. A child of this age might surprise you with a provocative question, such as why the teenager across the street uses drugs. Keep the answer short and simple. For instance, you might say, "John, I don't know why he wants to take drugs. I wish he would take care of his mind and body." Long detailed speeches on drugs (or other destructive behaviors) would not be fitting.

As children mature from ages 13 and up, discuss all (or most of) the chapters with them. Again, you need to determine their ability to handle the information and you need to avoid tiresome, repetitive lectures. Keep it loving and short. An English teacher would make sure that students studied the verb, but the teacher would not dwell on it once the class had grasped it. Try not to dwell on heavy subjects, either. Sell your children, instead, on the goodness of a moral life. "...He who does good is of God; he who does evil has not seen God." (3 John:11).

You may ask yourselves, "When can we find the time to discuss these topics with our children?" It will be different for each family. One family might find a few minutes for discussion before bedtime prayers, after reading books, during meals, or while traveling in the car. Others might find time before going to Mass on Sundays, after religious education, or before a volunteer project.

Other families might enjoy a weekly "Family Fun Time" with prayer, discussion from this book, and games. A mother of two small children told me she is eager for when she can begin regular fun time with her own family. She said, "Family Fun Time, when I was growing up, was among the best times we had." A good time to start this activity is when some of the children reach school age.

Family Fun Time can include games and activities such as, Ring-Around-the-Rosie, Button-Button-Who-Has-the-Button, checkers, or baseball depending on your children's ages. One father was amazed, though, when every child in the neighborhood wanted to join in on "Drop-the-Handkerchief." While teens can act standoffish, they usually enjoy participating in games with younger children. The less parents push, the more they cooperate. Ask the kids to help plan the fun times. Their ideas can be endless, so use time limits; one hour might be enough. Keep the learning time short, too. Make Family Fun Time about ten percent prayer and discussion, and then ninety percent fun at first. Have the younger ones go off and play if the discussion gets too advanced for them. Decide at the end of each session when you will meet again and what activity you will do the next time.

This book presents Church teaching and the natural consequence of certain behaviors. Faith and reason never oppose each other. Both are the criteria for sound decision-making. Ask the Holy Spirit to guide you in teaching your children. If you still have difficulty, consider that positive change comes in small increments. This takes time, prayer, and patience. Further help is available from the bibliography at end of each chapter, Catholic bookstores, teachers, priests, counselors, mental health workers, libraries, and various self-help groups. Make use of them; you won't be the only parent who needs extra help. The manner in which you parent your children carries into the second and third and tenth generations to come. This is an important vocation.

With just a few conversations in a month, children will be firmly rooted in their faith and pass it on for generations to come. This means that families have reason and fortitude to stay together, and that moms and dads can be committed to each other. It means that children will avoid peer pressure (well, mostly). It means that families can climb out of the dysfunctional environment of the self-centered, me-first, lust-filled, pagan attitudes around us. They can have dynamic families. They can put God first. They can trust marriage again, and they can understand pro-life.

Let your children know that God loves them, and energize them to know how to love Him back.

Chapter I

Cultivate Love and Self-worth

"First of all, I urge that supplications, prayers, intercessions, and thanksgivings be made for all men, for kings and all who are in high positions, that we may lead a quiet and peaceable life, godly and respectful in every way." (1 Timothy 2:1,2).

Children raised with faith and love gain self respect. They need this confidence to withstand temptations, whether or not the bad influence comes from movies, music, television, peer groups, friends, or family. We all have known people who during recent decades got themselves into deep trouble after acquiring a false self-esteem. Lacking, or in some cases rejecting, sound moral principles, their self-esteem meant self-gratification. Consequently, they harmed themselves as well as others.

Overwhelming are today's statistics for young people. Students are bullied. Alcohol, drugs, fornication, suicide, and violence are too high. Should we let frightening numbers discourage us? No, but we should be sobered by them, and rediscover the true meaning of self-esteem. Your parents and grandparents dealt with their own different, yet strikingly similar, set of concerns for their children: hunger, poverty, and war. Now we have expanded that also to mean hunger for love, poverty of mind, body, and soul, and war on self-worth and respect for life.

Your children's self-worth and respect develop when they know they are loved, and when they can love in return. This is one young mother's shocking tale: She said good night and "I love you" to her eleven-year-old boy, who became suddenly ill. She was startled as he responded, "Mom, I didn't know that you loved me." Could this be you? Could your child be one that didn't know you loved and kissed him as a baby, changed his diapers, and wiped his spills, fed him at 2:00 A.M., laughed when he uttered his first sentence, and cried as he marched to kindergarten? Be determined to show your children that you love them, and God

1

loves them too. Love is the essential element for getting young people to understand God's laws. They have to understand that God loves them, and that is why God gives them firm rules to follow. Obedience to his tough love keeps one out of trouble. If parents leave love and God out of the picture, then there is no reason for children to obey the law of life as pronounced in the Bible, in this book, or anywhere.

Cardinal Lopez Trujillo, president of the Vatican's Pontifical Council for the Family, said we all must grow in Christian maturity before we can pass this on to our children.[1] It begins with love. Therefore, this chapter deals with some Christian fundamentals: God is love; love and respect in the family; and work, determination, and goals. These basics of mature Christian living provide a solid foundation for your children's emerging visions of themselves and of their place in the world. Read each exercise (1,2, and so forth) to yourself first, and put it into your own words. Some parts take minutes; others take longer depending on the age of your children and the topic discussed.

(As you speak with your children, follow the instructions from the Introduction on the suitable age for each child.)

God's Love

Let your children know that God loves them, and energize them to love him back. Encourage your children to be close to our Lord. This is the most important step to keep them trouble-free and to help them make good decisions. Dare to put your children on the side of their Father in heaven.

1. Reflect on God's love

God wants your children to know he created and redeemed them because he loves them tremendously. The *Catechism of the Catholic Church* says this about his love for us:

> God, infinitely perfect and blessed in himself, in a plan of sheer goodness freely created man to make him share in his own blessed life. For this reason, at every time and in every place, God draws close to man. He calls man to seek him, to know him, to love him with all his strength. He calls together all men, scattered and divided by sin, into the unity of his family, the Church. To accomplish this, when the fullness of time had come, God sent his Son as Redeemer and Savior. In

his Son and through him, he invites men to become, in the Holy Spirit, his adopted children and thus heirs of his blessed life.[2]

Read or explain this Catechism passage to your children, and give your testimony of how you are trying to know, love, and serve God. When we worship God, we worship one as huge as the heavens above. He alone (not a trite devil) has the passport to happiness, here and hereafter. Share your hope to be an heir of the kingdom of heaven. Write below what you will say.

_____

_____

_____

This may appear to be the shortest exercise in the whole book, but loving and knowing God takes a lifetime. Repeat various ways to say the words, "God loves you, and I love you, too," often in the weeks, months, and years ahead.

2. Invigorate love for God

Grace is a supernatural blessing that God freely bestows on us for our eternal salvation. In turn, some ways we can reinvigorate our love for God are by praying to God, practicing self-denial, and serving others.

Pray to and love God

It is through prayer that we communicate with the God who loves us. Prayer isn't only kneeling and praying as we do in church—although praising God in this manner is important. Prayer also is keeping God in mind all the time. In prayer, we adore God. In prayer, we ask for help to do God's will. In prayer, we show our appreciation for God's goodness. In prayer, we ask forgiveness for our sins. Prayer opens us to God, allowing him to pour his spirit into our souls.

With your children, compose a prayer (of praise, petition, thanksgiving, or penance) for a good day and a prayer for help on a difficult day.

_____

_____

_____

The Church institutes sacramentals. They are sacred signs that help us pray and prepare for the sacraments and other significant times in our life. Sacramentals always embrace prayer and may include the laying on of hands, holy water, and sign of the cross. Sacramentals are objects, blessed and set apart by the Church to create an atmosphere of faith for us, such as: relics, Stations of the Cross, rosary, crucifix, statues, pictures, and so forth. (Find more on prayer and sacramentals in the, *Catechism of the Catholic Church,* p. 898 and #1667-79.) In what ways can your family make better use of sacramentals?

———————————————————————————

———————————————————————————

———————————————————————————

———————————————————————————

Help your children memorize some of the Church's most beloved prayers by saying them together before and after meals, and when arising and before bedtime at night. Refer to prayers in the back of the book.

The greatest commandment is to "love the Lord your God with all your heart, and with all your soul, and with all your might...." (Deuteronomy 6:5). God desires us to be on fire with his love. Think of what it would be like if Babe Ruth had never had a cheering section. What a dull game it would have been if everyone had stood around listlessly. So too, our faith seems boring and cheerless when lived without zeal. Recall a time in your life when some person or event inspired you with zeal for God: the reception of a sacrament, a family holiday, a retreat, the inspiring examples of a particular priest, religious brother or sister, teacher or friend.

———————————————————————————

———————————————————————————

———————————————————————————

Could your children benefit from such an experience? Are there ways in which their faith in God's love is being hindered that you as a parent can do something to change?

———————————————————————————

———————————————————————————

———————————————————————————

Practice self-denial

Fasting, abstinence, and other forms of self-denial are necessary for Christian maturity. They help us love and obey God for his own sake and not only for the good things that he gives us. They increase our compassion for the poor and suffering. They teach us to say no to ourselves and thereby grow in freedom from vices and bad habits. They also offer us opportunities to do penance for our sins and the sins of others. Children need regular practices of self-denial to gain the strength and freedom they need to resist peer pressure. If Terri gives up candy for Lent, wouldn't she be more likely to have the freedom to say "no" to far more serious temptations than candy? Lent, Advent, Fridays, and Sundays are excellent times to practice saying "no" to us and "yes" to God. The Church expects it. How would you explain the above to your children?

_____

_____

_____

Name a few acts of self-denial that have been growing experiences for you. Have these involved fasting and praying or giving of your time, talent, and money? Could any of these acts of self-denial be relevant for your children?

_____

_____

_____

Requiring small sacrifices of your children is one of the best things you can do for them.

Dr. Steven Glenn and Jane Nelsen, Ed. D. state in their book *Raising Self-Reliant Children In a Self-Indulgent World*, "In truth, pampering is one of the most unloving things we can do to our children."[3] A spoiled child with too many rules never followed and too many material goods never given up has a difficult time discovering how to be responsible for oneself and considerate of others.

If you always get what you ask for, why should you work for anything?

If someone bought, washed, and hung up your clothing all your life, why would you take care of it?

If you had a toy chest full of things you never shared, why would you be generous later in life?

If you drank as much soda as you wanted when you were six years old, why not drink twelve packs of beer when you become sixteen?

If you heard a resounding "yes" to your every desire as a child, how would you learn to say "no"?

If you broke family rules without consequences, how would you know if any rules and regulations in life were worth obeying?

With the advent of smaller families and in some cases more funds, many children are overwhelmed with excessive amounts of toys, money, clothes, comfort, and attention. Ways to protect your children from excessiveness and selfishness include:

* Give gifts according to need.

* Give gifts in your children's names to other children who are less fortunate.

* Make the words "Please" and "Thank you" some of their first mastered words, and say "You're welcome" as a follow-up.

* Repair old favorite toys and clothing instead of constantly buying new ones. Too many possessions, everywhere, destroy creativity and build confusion.

* Use allowance as a tool to learn the value of money, not as a gift to reward work efforts. Work should be done because you are a valuable member of the family.

* Buy only what you planned to buy and refuse to give in to whining children who want something extra on a shopping trip.

* Keep treats to a minimum, otherwise they are no longer treats.

* Refuse to feel guilty because other parents give their children more. For instance, when your child has a birthday party, ask that each child bring a dollar and it will be put into an account for the future, or it will be given to an orphanage.

* Clean out your closets, drawers, and chests each year and give items to the poor. If you haven't worn or used it in a year, you should consider giving it away.

* Make few rules, but expect your children to follow the ones you make.

* Make peace; take your family to the Sacrament of Reconciliation at least once a month. Get a copy of Mary Ann Budnik's book on confession in the bibliography.

Could some of the above suggestions help your family?

_____

_____

_____

We like to see shine on an apple, but the shine is not the whole apple. So too, we like to see our children as the shiny spots of our family, but they do not take the household's center stage as self-centered children do. Self-centered children appear to be in command. They control and change family rules to fit their wants and desires. They do not know the meaning of the phrase self-denial.

Serve God and neighbor

In *The Book of Virtues*, William J. Bennett writes, "Compassion…comes close to the very heart of moral awareness, to seeing in one's neighbor another self."[4] We love God when we love and have compassion for our associates in and outside of the family.

Jesus said what we do to others, we do also to him. Help your children understand they have a unique purpose in living, a special way they can use their time and talent to love others. Do this not because it makes your family feel better, but because it is good for others. Brothers, sisters, aunts, uncles, the aged, the poor, the hungry, the sick all have special needs we can help to satisfy. Here are some examples of things we can do:

* Help a brother or sister with homework.

* Forgive a sibling or classmate for some offense, realizing that God first forgave us.

* Become friends with lonely and withdrawn children at school.

* Help with a small project at church.

* Serve the poor at the local food pantry or soup kitchen.

* Visit the sick, elderly, and handicapped.

* Help a grandparent mow the lawn or clean the house.

* Contribute alms from their allowance or earnings.

* Help a pro-life cause and profess that all people are created by God and have dignity from the moment of their conception (i.e., moment of fertilization) until their natural death.

* Invite lonely individuals to your holiday dinners.

* Offer to take a friend or family member to church on Sunday with your family.

* Other_____

Brainstorm some other ways that your family can share God's love with others.

"Listen to me your father, O children; and act accordingly, that you may be kept in safety" (Sirach 3:1).

Love and Respect Within the Family

When Jesus said, "Let the children come to me...." (Matthew 19:14), the children received his love and respect. As parents, you can edify your children in a similar way by bringing them to Jesus through your example of tenderness and caring.

3. Give unconditional love

Children need to feel the security of our unconditional love, "If I speak in the tongues of men and of angels, but have not love, I am a noisy gong or a clanging cymbal" (I Corinthians 13: 1). Our unconditional love is like the love God has for us: it is absolute and limitless. God loves us not for anything we can do for him, but he loves us for our own sake. A parent's unconditional love for his children is similar to God's love for us. It is based not on the child's attributes or merits, but on his being a gift of God, created in God's image and likeness. Here are some ways we show our children that we love them unconditionally:

* Using encouraging words
* Respecting and enjoying each individual family member
* Bringing about family togetherness at meals, holidays, and special occasions
* Keeping our word
* Controlling our anger
* Being quick to forgive and ask for forgiveness
* Showing courtesy
* Giving generously of our time
* Correcting faults with gentleness
* Refraining from ridicule and criticism

Underline the strengths in your household and congratulate yourself. Then circle one or two areas that could be improved and discuss them with your family. There is a better way to say and do almost everything.

4. Help children to know and love themselves

"A loving person is a person who loves himself" says Leo F. Buscaglia. Jesus tells us to go even further and to love our neighbor as we love ourselves. We can portray affection through loving communication. These skills, however, are sadly lacking among many of this generation's children. A deficient home life, television, computers, and loud music all precipitate a lack of communication among family members. Make every effort to have good communication skills in your home, especially if family members seem angry, troubled, shy, or lonesome. Patient, positive responses and sharp listening skills produce good communication between parents and children. Tasteful, agreeable communications attract your children; sour communications chase them away. We can help children know and love themselves when we listen to them and give them gentle correction, consequences, and affirmation. "One catches more flies with a spoonful of honey than with twenty casks of vinegar," said St. Francis de Sales.

Listening

Children need your full attention when they talk to you. You, in turn, need to know you also have their regard when you talk to them. Ways we give someone our complete attention include:

* Turn off the TV, the CD player, and so forth, and tune into your children. Let them know nothing is more important for that moment.

* Listen without interrupting until they are finished.

* Make eye contact. When you have good eye contact, it suggests to the speaker that you listen with your ears.

* Repeat for clarification and understanding what *they* have just said.

* Ask them to repeat what *you* have just said. You then will know if they have received the message correctly.

* Use good body language such as touching, smiling, and sitting forward in your chair. Good body language shows your children that you are listening with care.

* Listen with a positive attitude.

* Empathize with your children. They need to know you understand their predicaments. Sometimes saying less is better. In their book, *How To Talk So Kids Will Listen & Listen So Kids Will Talk*, Adele Faber and Elaine Mazlish state that "Oh...umm..." or "I see" listening statements show your empathy. They said, "Words like these, coupled with a caring attitude, are invitations to a child to explore [their]...own thoughts and feelings, and possibly come up with [their] own solutions." Note the following similar example as to what Faber and Mazlish described:

Mom: I wish you weren't so angry.

Son: Well, I'm mad at sister because she took my airplane and didn't put it away.

Mom: Umm.

Son: I found it in the garage.

Mom: Oh, I see.

Son: I'm going to keep it in my room from now on, and ask her to put it away next time she borrows it.[5]

(Notice how her son worked out his own solution without having to be told or scolded.)

* Help your children define their feelings; "Sounds as if you are pretty happy about getting that A-plus," or "You seem upset about this situation." It is good to express feelings, but here is a helpful consideration regarding negative feelings. When your children are sharing *bad* feelings, keep talking until positive feelings and attitudes are in sight, otherwise children become discouraged. They might think it's okay to wallow in bad feelings and fall prey to brooding, self-pity, or wrong solutions. "[D]o not let the sun go down on your anger...." (Ephesians 4:26).

Recall if there was an instance when either you or someone you knew didn't listen properly to what had been said. Were any skills noted above lacking from that conversation?

_____

_____

_____

Circle any skills noted above that you might want to practice with, and relate to, your children.

Try to reserve a special time every day to spend with each of your children. Learn to exchange the glad and sad, the exciting and dull, the cheerful and fearful events of the day. This helps you practice your listening skills, it helps you form a close relationship with your children, and it helps you exchange ideas about problems, morals, and a host of other important matters.

Correcting

When children have done something wrong, begin by asking questions such as those beginning with "what," "where," "how," and "when," to let your child share thoughts, feelings, and actions with you. Again, they might discover their own solution to a situation with your guidance. Questions asked in a patient, respectful way help children to think things through and to make good decisions. There is a note of warning, though; you may want to avoid "why" questions, as these tend to sound too interrogating. Often, children don't know why they do things wrong. Instead, focus questions more on the present and future than on the past. Rather than say, "Why did you mess the living room with your toys?" say, "Where will you put these toys?"

When your children have answered a question, base your response on solid facts, reasonable expectations, and choices. Jim Fay, director of Love and Logic Institute says, "...make sure that the kid has to make some choices, some alternatives. Would you rather do it now, would you rather do it later, would you rather do this, would you rather do that. But always the choices will come out so that no matter which way the kid chooses, the parent is going to be deliriously happy..."[6] The parent is happy, not the child. For example, you ask your son where he is going and he says, "to the mall," when you specifically told him to go to the grocery store. You could deal with facts and expectations to set his path straight by using, "I want," "I expect," "I need," "I insist," and "fact" statements. For example, "I want you to go to the grocery store because we need bread and you agreed to go. Do you want to go now or in half an hour?"

Here are examples of questions followed by positive "I" or "fact" statements and choices.

* "What do you plan to do about the lamp you broke?" Listen and then if the problem isn't solved, say, "I expect you to take responsibility for the accident by offering to help fix it or pay for its replacement."

* "How do you plan to get this composition done?" Listen... "Large projects are more easily accomplished when broken into smaller parts. Do you want to do it all tonight or leave some for morning?"

* "When do you plan to come home?" Listen... "I need you home in time for dinner at 6:30. Would you want to come home at 6:00 or 6:30"

* "How do you plan to tell your sister your are sorry?" Listen... "I need you to go to time out so you can cool down. Do you want it to be on the rocker or on your bed?"

For practice, here are some ineffective statements that shut kids right up. Write in some questions followed by positive "I" or "fact" statements instead.

* I suppose you'll be home late as usual.

_____

_____

_____

* You flunked math!

_____

_____

_____

* Why can't you get good grades like your brother?

_____

_____

_____

* Aren't you ever going to get this done?

_____

_____

_____

* I can never find you when I need you!

_____

_____

_____

You can correct a child sometimes only by listening and giving choices and expectations, as above. Other times you must resort to consequences. Again, handle it with courtesy. A key to good conversation is kindness. In the book *That's Not What I Meant*, Deborah Tannen, Ph.D., says, "...We balance them [rules of politeness and kindness] all to be appropriately friendly without imposing, to keep appropriate distance without appearing aloof."[7] You can relay corrective information to your children in two ways: with kindness or without kindness. Choose kindness.

When you relay information harshly, it only reminds children about something they already know is wrong, and they probably feel ashamed of it. Such statements as: "You should know better," or "You drive like a maniac," or "That's stupid," are hurtful, ineffective, and often counterproductive.

In contrast, when you avoid scolding and relay truly useful and detailed information, it tells children what they need to know in an understanding and compassionate way. You inspire them to do better.

Use "I want," "I expect," "I need," "I insist," and "fact" statements, as above. If you have a spouse, occasional "We" statements are even better. "We" statements show children that you and your spouse have a united front. Then use reasonable explanations about why you care so much. Follow with consequences that you as a parent will do, and not something the child will do. In addition, the consequence should make the parent happy. Use "I will" or "We will" consequences. Examples follow:

* "We want you to drive the car slower, because we love you *so much* and want you to arrive home in one piece. Since you didn't obey us, we will keep the keys to the car for three full days."

* "We expect good behavior at school, because we want you to learn. Since you disobeyed in class, we think you must be too tired to study; therefore, we will turn the lights out fifteen minutes earlier each night this week, so that you get more sleep."

* "I insist that you pick up the clothing in your room, so that items don't get destroyed or lost. The family rule is that clothes need to be put away properly. I only buy clothes for kids who take good care of them. Since you didn't hang the clothes up, I will have to stop buying you new ones until you can learn to care for what is yours."

Notice how parents have full use of the car for three days, they save on electricity, and they don't have to buy expensive clothing because of the consequences they presented to their child. The *parent* is happy!

Recall a conflict you and your children may have had, and think of polite "I" or "we" statements, reasonable "fact" explanations, and "I (we) will" consequences you either used, or could have used in response.

_____

_____

_____

Heat not a furnace for your foe so hot that it do singe yourself.—Shakespeare, *Henry VIII*

Affirming

Children like to discover their uniqueness, both their strengths and their weaknesses. They want to grow in truth about themselves with our loving help. We can all recall times when someone affirmed us for something we either did or said; we know how good it made us feel. When someone related positive statements such as, "I like your room," "I appreciated the help," and "We worked harder today than yesterday." It made you want to do even better the next time. Most likely, you wouldn't have let down a gracious person for anything.

Recall special skills or traits each child possesses and ask other members to add to it. Be genuine, your children know when you are false or insincere. Avoid superlatives such as, "You're the *best* wrestler." Such messages tend to generate self-centered or negative responses such as, "I am not," "You're just saying that" or "Yeah, I am the best."

Child 1

_____

_____

_____

Child 2

_____

_____

_____

Child 3

_____

_____

_____

Child 4

_____

_____

_____etc.

5. Nurture positive relationships among siblings

Children build friendships among their own brothers and sisters when they have good feelings about who they are among their siblings. One way to insure those good feelings is to avoid unfair comparisons of brothers and sisters. Statements such as, "Mike started walking at ten months, but Kyle never started until he was one year," and "Tim almost ran the four minute mile, but Kent will never make it," cause jealousy, rivalry, and resentment among brothers and sisters. Such comparisons do not lead to a healthy self-knowledge. Think of a time in your youth when you were unfairly distinguished from someone in your family. What words would you have liked to have heard instead?

_____

_____

To help build a sense of camaraderie among your children, ask them to pick a task, such as one below, and do it in the following week.

* When dividing a cake, for instance, ask one child to cut two pieces, and then let another pick the first piece.
* As a team, help clean each other's mess.
* Ask older children to rock and soothe the baby.
* Help plan a family event or vacation together.
* Other_____

Children who learn to love and respect their brothers and sisters consequently show love and respect to others outside the home.

Friendships among siblings generally grow as children mature. Often later in life, they are among one's best friends, while so many other friends drift away. Now is the time you can build that bond, when your family is young.

6. Find private, peaceful places for children

Think, for a moment how you would feel if you traveled to a meeting and no one offered you a chair. You might feel as if you didn't belong. Likewise, children need a place they identify as their own: an area somewhat free of noise and interference to think, daydream, create, and pray. Their hideout need not be a room of their own: it could be a bed with a place to store belongings, a desk that is clutter-free, a space devoid of a deluge of possessions, or even a corner with a special chair. Recall in your youth if you either did or didn't have an area in your house that was especially your territory. How did you feel about it?

_____

_____

_____

Having a space of one's own does not mean it is devoid of orderliness, cleanliness, and even holiness. Discuss how you could provide your children with spaces of their own.

_____

_____

_____

One would be in less danger
From the wiles of the stranger
If one's own kin and kith
Were more fun to be with.

—Ogden Nash, "Family Court"

Work, Determination, and Goals

Parents and children can discover the rewards of working together and contributing to the common good of the family by sharing the tasks involved in running the household. The very foundation for their learning begins in the home. They acquire real skills, as well as self-esteem, self-confidence, consideration for the needs of others, and a strong work ethic.

7. Assign age-appropriate chores

Children want to feel needed and useful almost as much as adults do. Even children as young as two and three feel a sense of pride in themselves when they "help Mommy." Very young children are capable of working, provided it is scaled down to fit their size and limitations. Putting away toys, wiping the tabletop, sorting clean socks, slicing bananas, and clearing one's plate from the table are only a few things three to five-year-olds can do. From about six years, children can make their beds, fold laundry, set the table, dust, and so forth. As children become teenagers, they need work that is more challenging, although they may resist it. Tasks teens can perform include painting and caulking the house, replacing a fence post, cleaning a bathroom, sweeping cobwebs, changing the car's oil filter, mowing the lawn, grilling a steak, washing dishes, cooking a meal, shopping for healthful groceries, sewing a button, balancing a checkbook, and doing laundry. Such jobs help them to see themselves as capable and dependable.

If Kim has confidence in the way she helped Mom paint the living room, she will carry herself as a "can-do" person and be less intimidated by the gifts or ability of others. If Jason refurbished a doorstep with his father, Jason will see that his father has confidence in his talent to perform as an adult.

Children who have real work to do suffer less from a destructive form of idleness that leads too many young people into trouble. Think about this for a minute. Would you expect a troubled youth to tell you he had worked at responsible jobs and had known adults who had a great deal of confidence in him?

Make a list of tasks around the house that you can delegate to your children.

Children cannot perform a chore until you first give them the necessary training. Outline the steps needed to prepare children for the work you intend them to do. Remember that perfection will not be attained at first. Give your children the supervision and opportunity for practice that they need before expecting them to get it right, even if they are sixteen! This is special bonding time. This is important, even if you have other smaller children that need your attention too. All children deserve one-on-one time with a parent.

8. Talk about social skills

Children can develop good social skills to acquire and maintain their friendships. Kevin who hasn't mastered the art of eating spaghetti will face terrific embarrassment when he eats it for the first time at an elegant Italian restaurant. Jan who never excuses herself when she wants to break into a conversation will wonder why friends shun her when she wants them to listen to her. Learning courteous manners takes practice. Teach your children good social skills in the following ways:

* Practice making introductions with your children so that they will know how to introduce themselves to new friends. For example, excuse yourself if you are standing in a group and shake someone's hand, smile, and say, "Hi! How are you? I'm _____. What class are you in?" Handshaking is a learned skill. Show your children how to wrap their hand and thumb around yours, squeeze slightly, and give a good, firm shake.

* Show your children how to negotiate: "I'd like to play baseball. What would you like to play? We could play your game now, and mine in an hour. What do you think?"

* Practice good etiquette at the family dinner table. Show children how to serve others first, to pass the food without reaching across the table, to place a napkin on their lap, to eat difficult foods, to chew quietly, and so forth.

* Try to plan schedules so that you can eat meals together as often as possible. On occasion, invite grandparents, other relatives, and friends to your house for meals and encourage children to enter the conversation. This way, they learn the art of getting to know others, especially adults. This does not mean, however, that children should speak out of turn and dominate the conversation. Children must understand they are not the focus of attention in the family. Psychologist John

Rosemond said, "…a child who is raised at the center of his parents' attention cannot develop true respect for them. He cannot, therefore, develop either respect for others or genuine self-respect."[8]

* Limit television viewing and computer games to only a few hours a week so that your children discover other activities that include family and friends, such as board games, card games, Ping-Pong, and the like.

* Have children repeat the words, "Excuse me," and "I'm sorry," often. A child who learns to take responsibility for a given offense will have reciprocating friends. Likewise, help your children learn to give pardon with such expressions as "I forgive you," and "It's okay; we all make mistakes."

* Play games with your children and let them lose occasionally. In this way, they learn how to deal with defeat. Show them how much fun you can have, but show them it's not fun if someone is a poor loser.

* Teach your children how to give sincere compliments to others. Be an example; admire others for their goodness.

Circle the social skills you want to share with your children.

9. Discuss self-consciousness

Children, especially twelve-to fourteen-year-olds, are often self-conscious about their appearance. Self-conscious children tend to follow the crowd and yield to peer pressure. Therefore, let your children know they are of special value because of their humility, gentleness, kindness, and other virtues; and not because of either their physical beauty or their material possessions.

Consider the words of this young man who received honors from fellow classmates. He said, "I couldn't figure out why they elected me class president. The only thing I did was open doors for people." Humility, gentleness, and kindness were the reasons for his admiration by the students. Physical and material gifts are wonderful, but fleeting. In and of themselves, they do not add one iota to a person's character. The most admired people are the ones who have eyes not upon themselves, but upon the good they do for others. Make a list of people you admire with your children, then ask yourselves what qualities of theirs you esteem the most.

_____

_____

_____

_____

_____

_____

_____

_____

Recall if there was an instance in your childhood when you were self-conscious about your appearance. Was there a time when you didn't like your haircut, or you thought your shoes were out of fashion, or you felt too fat, too short, or too tall? What helpful statement did you hear (or want to hear) from your parents?

_____

_____

To help children appreciate their own virtues, try comments such as: "Thanks for listening to what I had to say." "You were so patient with your baby brother." "It was thoughtful of you to pick me these flowers." What soothing statements similar to the suggestions above would your children like to hear?

_____

_____

How could you ask your children to be kind toward others about their attire, disability, or physique?

_____

_____

10. Put sports into perspective

One way for children to build their confidence, as well as make friends, is through sports. When children participate, they need mild affirmation for cooperating, instead of criticism for losing the athletic event. Too much competitive emphasis and too much criticism causes cheating, jealousy, perfectionism, and low self-esteem. Recall an instance when you tried your hardest and someone found fault with what you did in a competition. Chances are, the criticism did not help. Negative people seldom help you or your children improve.

Together, with your children, write either an "I" or "fact" comment you would rather have heard in a particular faultfinding incident. Example: "That was a tough catch."

_____

_____

_____

On the other end of the spectrum, excessive award for good performance gives children the message that they are not worthy unless they receive rewards. As with excessive criticism, excessive award causes cheating, jealousy, perfectionism, and low self-esteem, also.

Competitive sports are good for adolescents, but for younger children (and adolescents, too), encourage the unstructured kind for them when possible. Unstructured play, where adults are near when needed but not directly supervising the activity, helps children gain self-worth. Competition also helps them gain integrity, and ability, as well as the capacity to do something for no other reason than the fun of it.

11. Set goals

Children need help in setting goals. These goals, however, should not be so high that the chance of failure prevents them from trying. Children with goals have a vision for the future: they are not as likely to spoil their plans and dreams with dangerous choices (drugs, sex, and crime) in the present.

Ways to communicate with children about the importance of their futures include:

* Open an educational savings account and encourage them (after tithing to charity) to put a portion of their money from work, allowances, and gifts into the bank. No matter what they do in life, they will likely need either higher education or technical training.

* Choose good schools from the start: consider Catholic ones and homeschool. Find homeschooling and Catholic college information in the bibliography at the end of this chapter. Refuse to push children into stressful competitive and achievement situations they are not prepared to handle.

* Help your children discover and develop their true talents of body, mind, and soul.

* Encourage your children's interests by giving them books about these things for birthdays and other special occasions.

* Refuse to be negative when a lack of talent exists in one area. Say, for example, "Reading might not be coming easily right now, but it will click, and in the meanwhile look how well you do in math."

* Show interest in school activities and homework, visit the classroom and attend parent-teacher meetings. Show positive attitudes toward the competence

of faculty. Studies show that students' grades improve when parents have confidence in their child's teachers.

* Visit the library and find books on great people and subjects that are of interest to your children. Make learning fun and relaxed.

* Teach life skills at home such as map reading, list-making, orderliness, money management, time management, and especially spirituality. These skills will help them no matter what they do in life.

* Be a good adult role model in your occupation whether at home or at work.

* Discuss various job opportunities. Show them job sites and encourage participation in part-time jobs.

* Pray for children to discover their vocations, whether these are vocations to marriage and parenting, the single life, or the priesthood and religious life. Ask your children to pray that they discern their vocation with the assistance of God.

* Instead of nagging teens to go to school, ask them what they want to do in five or ten years. Ask questions such as: "What will happen if you don't continue your education?" "What will you do if you can't find a full-time job?" "How will you buy a car?" "How will you support a family?" and "How will you convince an employer that you will be punctual if you continue to skip school?" By asking questions, you force your children to think about what is good for their welfare. Your goal is to point them in the right direction.

Relate some instances that helped you as a child gain an interest in your future.

_____

_____

_____

Circle any ideas, above, you want to discuss with your children. Find *The Life Work Inventory* by Rick Sarkistan, Ph. D. in the bibliography.

The lofty goals we set for our children do not matter. What does matter is the service they do for God and neighbor with the talents they have. God's gift to us is our life, and our gift to God is what we do with it.

Endnotes:

1. Cardinal Lopez Alfonso Lopez Trujillo interview reported by Charlie Wieser, "Society needs 'mature Christian faith'," Omaha (CNS), *West Nebraska Register* (1 Nov 91): n.p.

2. *Catechism of the Catholic Church* (Washington, D.C.: United States Catholic Conference, 1997), Publication no. 5-110, #1, p. 7.

3. Dr. Steven Glenn and Jane Nelsen Ed. D., *Raising Self-Reliant Children in a Self-Indulgent World* (California: Prima Publishing & Communications, 1988), p. 125.

4. William J. Bennett, *The Book of Virtues* (New York: Simon & Schuster, 1993), p. 107.

5. Adele Faber and Elaine Mazlish, *How To Talk So Kids Will Listen & Listen So Kids Will Talk* (New York, NY: Avon Books, 1980), p. 13.

6. Fay, Jim, *Helicopters, Drill Sergeants and Consultants*, cassette or CD (Colorado: Love and Logic Institute, Inc., 1992).

7. Deborah Tannen, Ph.D., *That's Not What I Meant* (New York: William Morrow and Co. Inc., 1986), p. 37.

8. John Rosemond, psychologist, *Knight-Ridder Newspapers*, as cited in "The Three R's Ideas on Child-rearing Not New," *Grand Island [NE] Independent* (n.d.): n.p.

Bibliography:

Bennett, W. J. *The Book of Virtues*. New York: Simon & Schuster, 1993.

By Way of the Family Your Complete Resource for discount homeschool materials. Saint Paul, MN 55101: 1090 Payne Avenue. Telephone: 1-800-588-2589, local: 651-778-0287, Web site: www.bywayofthefamily.com.

Budnik, Mary Ann. *Raise Happy Children Series, Looking for peace? Try Confession!* and other books. Springfield, IL 62704: R.B. Media, Inc., 154 Doral, Telephone: 1-217-546-5261, Fax: 217-546-0558, Web site: www.rbmediainc.com.

Catholic Home Educator, provides support and resources to Catholic homeschoolers. Montrose, AL 36559: P.O. Box 787.

Faber, Adele and Elaine Mazlish. *How to Talk so Kids Will Listen and Listen so Kids Will Talk.* New York: The Hearst Corporation, 1980.

Family Life Center Publications, for information on Catholic colleges. Port Charlotte, FL 33949: P.O. Box 6060.

Fay, Jim. Helicopters, Drill Sergeants and Consultants, cassette on parenting. Golden, Colorado: Love and Logic Press. Telephone 1-800-338-4065, Website: www.loveandlogic.com. 1992.

Hahn, Kimberly and Mary Hasson. *Catholic Education: Homeward Bound,* a useful guide to Catholic homeschooling. San Francisco: Ignatius Press, 1996.

Homework Resources. Web site: www.studyweb.com.

Kippley, Sheila M. "Home Schooling Information Packet." Cincinnati, OH 45211: Couple to Couple League, P.O. Box 111184, Telephone: 513-471-2000, (orders only) call 1-800-745-8252, Fax: 513-557-2449, Web site: www.ccli.org.

Lockwood, Robert P., publisher. *Catholic Parent,* magazine. Huntington, IN: Our Sunday Visitor, Telephone 1-800-348-2440, Fax 1-219-356-8472, Web site: www.osv.com.

McDonald, Deacon Dr. Bob. *The Catholic Family.* Santa Barbara, CA: Queenship Publishing, 1999.

Mothers at Home, newsletter, books, and information. Non-profit organization providing support and encouragement to parents. Fairfax, VA: Telephone: 1-703-866-4164.

NACHE, Homeschooling for the New Millennium. Telephone: 1-410-379-6558, Web site: www.nache.org.

Rose, Michaels. *St. Joseph Messenger,* monthly reader for Catholic children and families. Cincinnati, OH 45211: St. Joseph Messenger, P.O. Box 11260, Telephone: 1-513-661-7009, Web site: www.stjoseph@erinet.com.

Rosemond, John. *Assuming the Power of Parenthood,* video. Gastonia, NC 28054-0020: Parent Power Productions, Inc., Center for Affirmative Parenting, P.O. Box 4124, 1993.

Sarkistan, Rick, Ph D. "The LifeWork Inventory," helps you make Christ-centered choices far beyond college and career. Telephone 1-888-297-4300, Web site www.lifeworkpress.com.

At different ages, children need discipline in different
forms and amounts.

Chapter II

Care and Discipline

'...[Y]ou that are younger be subject to the elders. Clothe yourselves, all of you, with humility toward one another, for "God opposes the proud, but gives grace to the humble"' (1 Peter 5:5).

How would the armed forces hold up without discipline? They would not. They would not even be able to move a group of troops from point A to point B. While the family is not the military, it is a human organization in need of discipline to function. A "dysfunctional" family is one where there is a lack of loving discipline, beginning with one or both parents being unable to discipline themselves. At different ages, children need discipline in different forms and amounts. The one-year-old responds well to a parent who diverts his attention. On the other end of the spectrum, a teenager responds to conversation, along with some trial and error. All ages, though, respond to loving authority and leadership from their parents.

Use this chapter for your own purposes or as a means to teach about parental responsibility to teenagers. Young people of this age need to learn how much patience it takes to be a good parent before they marry and have children. They also need to learn about parental reliability before they baby-sit.

The *Catechism of the Catholic Church* says, "The relationships within the family bring an affinity of feelings, affections and interests, arising above all from the members' respect for one another...."[1]

Beginning Discipline

As soon as children begin to sit up and crawl, they begin to demonstrate their little wills. Parents need to childproof their homes, use diversions, and respond to their unmet needs.

12. Childproof the home

Babies, of course, do not understand the pain of hot stoves, the shock from electrical outlets, and the germs on clumps of dirt. They require twenty-four-hour care.

Older children need to be aware that they must help to ensure their younger brother's and sister's safety, or any small child's safety in your home. Maintaining an orderly home keeps your family safe and saintly.

Look at your surroundings and view it from the eyes of a small child. Make a list of items in your house, such as extension and curtain cords, play equipment, sharp objects, stair steps, chemicals, poison plants, table cloths, and so on, that you could make less hazardous for small children living in or visiting your home.

_____

_____

_____

Dusting and vacuuming each week keep most dangerous items from tabletops and floors, and give families the satisfaction of a clean and saintly home.

13. Use diversions

Babies need to be redirected to better behaviors; for example, divert the two-year-olds' attention, instead of letting them scream for ten minutes because they don't want to sit on the potty. Lure them in the first minute with a book or toy, and if they are not interested tell them, "We'll come back later." It's important for parents to be united and win the wars, not with aggression, but with peace and discipline. Give them attention when they are good. This positive attention produces mature personalities in children. The two-year-old will be back on the potty twenty minutes later thinking it's a fun thing to do.

Children who do something bad to gain attention may need you to help them cure their insatiable curiosity. If two-year-old Matthew wants to climb on kitchen cupboards let him help you make cookie dough, in a safer spot of course. Other times you will pick them up and head in another direction. Still other times, you will need to put locks on cupboard doors so that they will not have access to hazardous substances. This takes time and patience.

In what ways could you avert a two-year-old, for instance, who liked to eat paper wads?

_____

_____

_____

Young children need a watchful eye and quick action.

14. Needs of small children

Some unpleasant behaviors at this age result from unmet needs for food, rest, and physical affection.

<u>Food</u>: Instead of bottle-feeding your babies, breast-feed them, if you can, for togetherness and good health. Your doctor will provide you with a list of foods they can eat in a few months. When children start eating table food (age one or so), choose fresh, frozen, or canned fruits and vegetables (fresh and frozen are best if they can handle the texture) for better health. Avoid foods that contain additives and excessive salt. Sit them in a high chair and let them put it into their mouths with their hands or a spoon. Since they put everything into their mouths (dirt and bugs included!) at this age, it is easy for them to learn to eat *good* food. Avoid entire diets of sweets or commercial baby foods, because foods such as these do not teach them to eat regular food as everyone else does. Let them practice on mashed table food, if the doctor allows. In this way, they will not be finicky eaters later when they are four and five. Eventually, they learn to eat the sour and bland, and even gradually with spoons in a civilized manner. Food groups include: whole-grain cereals, breads and brown rice; milk products; five or more servings of vegetables and fruits (darkest red, yellow, orange, green, and blue are highest in nutrition); and eggs, beans, lean poultry, fish, and meats. For fats, choose essential fatty acids for good health and brain function (check with local health food stores and some grocery stores). Follow your doctor's advice on allowing certain foods or groups of food, and ask how much each child needs according to age, height, weight, and activity.

<u>Rest</u>: Your doctor will also tell you about rest required for a child. Remember though, when they seem most wound-up and obnoxious, that may be when they need quiet time and a diversion to a good book before bedtime. A half-hour of quiet time before a night's rest gives you ample time to talk about the day's activities, and helps them settle down. It also gives you time with your spouse, and

gives you and them (depending if they are old enough) time to straighten the house for a new day ahead.

Physical, spiritual affection: Children need love, hugs, security, and faith. Children take time, and they respond to kindness. When they cry, they need you. If they cry more than a minute or two, they have a need. They don't need a lot of things, but they do need a lot of your time. Rock them to sleep, feed them, or change their diapers. They cry because they need something that you can give them. The love you give them now remains with them forever. Children need you. They need a mom with a shining home and a dad with a stable job. If you *need* day care, make sure children are in safe, loving environments, and are not kept in beds six hours a day. They deserve better.

Explain to young adults the responsibility, patience, and time involved in caring for their future children.

Discipline Ages Three to Five

Children ages three to five need alternatives, directives, and other corrections.

15. Give enough attention

Most three-to five-year-olds either do not know right from wrong, or they do something naughty to gain your attention. Avoid calling undue attention to negative behavior at this age or you will only get more of it.

Instead, point out the good behavior called for. Use "I" and "fact" statements and calmly divert their attention away from the negative and into the one or two positive alternatives. Use statements like the following:

* Tammy, I need peace and quiet, now. You can play with some play-dough while Mommy makes an important telephone call.

* Aaron, I know it's nice to build with blocks, but throwing them is not safe. Either stop throwing them, or let's pick them up and go outside.

* Trent, I do not like hearing naughty words. I want you to stay right here (example: chair, bed, porch) until you can talk nicely to your brother. (Some psychologists say the time-out should be one minute per year of child, but slightly extend the time if they are not behaving.) Then we will talk about using better words, and we will tell him you are sorry.

* Suzanne, it's bedtime. Let's put on your pajamas and brush your teeth. Do you want to read a story now or after you are ready for bed?

After misbehaving, a child may need attention later. One young mother said:

> "I could always tell when one of my five children felt neglected, lonely, or bad. They would be the one in trouble for some minor infraction. After the discipline was over as above, I always made it a point to go back to that child about an hour later and give a little extra undivided time, *totally separate* from the infraction. By giving this child special attention later, I seldom saw the bad behavior fester itself again."

The small child's feelings and resentments melt with a little undivided attention, love, and consonance.

16. Use alternatives

Children need constructive things to do. If three-year-old Megan wants to climb on the kitchen chairs, teach her to set the table in a safe way. If four-year-old Cole tinkers with every tool Dad owns, let him pound and saw with safe tools on some boards of his own. If two-year-old Thomas plays with television buttons, find something else that is safe to assemble and take apart. Learn to recognize the difference between a naughty child and one who may show tendencies toward his life profession at this tender age. Our future parents, cooks, carpenters, and engineers start this way.

Young children need personal attention from their parents *every day*. A half-hour spent with a three-year-old is time well spent, and will give the parent several hours to do whatever needs doing without being interrupted by misbehavior.

Have you had young children that misbehaved? _____ If so, how did you handle it?

_____

_____

_____

Were you satisfied with the results?_____If no, how could you have either diverted your children's attention with alternative activity or with "I" and "fact" statements that produce positive behaviors in them?

_____

_____

17. Spanking versus time-out, and communication

Some psychologists say that gentle spanking, without rage and *only* on the child's bottom, is okay; or at least, it's better than verbal abuse to get the child to mind, as when they are in grave danger. Still, spanking as an alternative to verbal abuse (or even to show control, disapproval, or authority) seems weak reason to spank. If you do spank, it should not be with anger, frustration, or desire to hurt.

Good reasons exist not to spank. Greg Popcak in his Catholic parent's book, *Parenting with Grace* gives ten reasons why we should not spank our children. Some reasons he gave are the following: "Jesus' own example was discipline, *not* punishment," "Scripture does not support spanking," "Spanking is violence," "Catholic luminaries in child-rearing oppose spanking."[2]

Better ways exist to discipline. There is no need to spank a child who appears to be naughty. Spanking a naughty three-year-old and then having an angry look on your face tells your child this is the way to act when one is mad. Instead, for instance, when Mandy screams and hollers in disappointment at the grocery store because she wants bubble gum, quiz her if she brought money for bubble gum. Explain to her that your money is to buy groceries. If she wants a treat, she needs to bring her own money. Say to her, "Let's look at how much it costs. It costs twenty-five cents. Next time we come, you bring twenty-five cents." If she continues the uproar, stay calm, and administer the time-outs, conversations, and discipline; and speak of repentance at the store just as you would at home. Your children may be aggressive in any instance, but check first, they also may be hungry or tired.

Communication, time-out, discipline, and contrition are what a child needs, but not aggression from the parent: (1) There is never need to call children names, such as liar, ungrateful, sneaky, spoiled, messy, dumb, and so on. These labels may very well carry with them throughout their lives and turn into self-fulfilling prophecies. (2) When you spank, it teaches children what they do other times is all right as long as they are not spanked. (3) When you spank and use course language, it teaches kids that they are no good, and that aggression is okay if you are an adult. Reason and change of heart, on the other hand, give them cause not to do misdeeds again.

Discipline for Older Children

Older children need good example, communication, and privileges either granted or removed depending on behavior.

18. Set limits

The adult world is full of limits and regulations, and it is no different for children. The time to start teaching about limits is when they are young—well before they are seven. Psychologists seem to agree that basic personality forms by the time children are this age. It doesn't mean, however, that you should stop teaching them after they reach a magic number.

If you haven't already, write down some rules you need at your house. Be sparing with rules, though, because too many can cause aggression, just as too few can cause irresponsibility.

Respect for parents_____
Respect for brothers and sisters_____
Chores_____
Homework_____
Television and computer_____
Whereabouts_____
Other_____

Rules need to be reasonable, such as: "No basketball until homework is finished," "Chores must be done before recreation on weekends," "We eat dinner as a family on the following weekdays…," and "Brothers and sisters who fight will be sent to separate rooms, so that mom and dad don't have to listen to the uproar."

19. Communicate with pre-teens

You cannot set rules, walk away, and expect obedience. Children understand better what is expected of them if you explain the rules and the consequences for breaking them. The following format may help you handle rules at your house:

(a) State the rule with love and concern, give your reasons, and listen to what your child has to say. Some children express themselves verbally; others may draw pictures and write down their thoughts and feelings. Children learn hundreds of mistaken ideas from media, friends, and so on. Tune in to them and determine where they stand on a particular obligation. The more communication you have with them the better. Do not let yourself be swayed by their whims. *Stick* to your principles.

(b) Ask the children to repeat the rule.

(c) State the consequences that will result from breaking the rule. Possibly, have your children help you determine the consequences. Be careful, though, they may surprise you and be harder on themselves or each other than you want them to be. Make the punishment something you can carry out. Avoid making rules that you have no intention of following through. When you later have to recant on such threats your children get the message that you are weak and incompetent. Refer to Exercise 4 on consequences.

(d) From time to time, when your child obeys a rule, make an affirmative comment such as, "Thank you for doing those chores," "Wow, the homework is done already!" "Thanks for not relying on the television so much," or "I'm happy I knew where you were."

Steps (a), (b), and (c) might go something like this, "It is not safe for you to be outside after dark; therefore, I want you to come home by eight o'clock." Pause, listen, explain, and repeat yourself if necessary. Ask the child to repeat the rule. Then say, "If you obey me tonight, then I can trust you to go to your friend's house tomorrow." Maintain your composure, *keep calm*, even if they become aggressive. You are in charge, not your children. Young people taught to be responsible for their actions are on the pathway to responsible adulthood. For practice, pick a rule from above (chores, homework, etc.) and use steps (a), (b), and (c) to write the way you might verbalize it.

_____

_____

_____

_____

_____

_____

After you verbalize steps (a), (b), and (c) above, what affirmative comment from step (d) could you give when your children imitate your rule?

_____

_____

20. Grant and withdraw privileges

Although God wants us to be like him, he also recognizes that we learn by our errors. Children are no different. Peek into your own childhood and find how you grew stronger after making a mistake. Your children, too, can grow wiser by facing the results of their own missteps. John Rosemond, family psychologist, says, allow your children to fail occasionally. Case in point: If a science project is late because your child has been irresponsible and waited until the last minute, refuse to pull him out of his mess (you might help later at *your* convenience, such as getting supplies at the store) and let him suffer the consequences. In fact, if your child doesn't get a bad grade after being irresponsible, be disappointed in the teacher! Rosemond says, "That's how you motivate children."[3]

At the left, list blunders you have made, and on the right, list the lessons in life (accountability, self-control, maturity, and so on) that you learned from that negative experience. Example: "My dad told me not to climb on the car, but when no one looked, I did it anyway. I fell and gouged a hole in my leg, therefore, I learned that I had better listen to Dad next time, so he wouldn't get in trouble with Mom!"

_____   _____

_____   _____

_____   _____

_____   _____

_____   _____

_____   _____

One saint pronounced that if you understood how much good comes from the tough times, you would pray for a few problems to come into your life. The tough times bring not only teachable lessons, but also laughable moments and cemented relationships. Learn to relish the tough times. Inform your children about how to handle failure. Teach them humility and how to correct their mistakes, and teach them how to rejoice, too.

A mother told this story. Her six-and eight-year-old boys played with the neighbors outside just before supper, and she gave them instructions to stay close to the house. "It's muddy elsewhere, and we're eating in five minutes," she said. (Note: asking the boys to repeat what she said may have produced better results.)

Soon she called from the doorstep. They heard her, but they didn't come. Instead of nagging, she and her husband sat down to eat without them. Fifteen minutes later, the boys rollicked home with mud from head to foot. They dropped their coats at the back door and tracked their muddy selves all the way to the kitchen table. Trying to maintain her composure, Mom whipped out a notebook and contemplated aloud, "Let me see, it looks like, since you didn't obey me, this is going to cost you, because everything is expensive. I'll have to make out your bill." The wide-eyed boys listened. "Your dinner is cold, and it will cost to heat it up again. Your clothes are dirty, and I will use much soap, water, and electricity to wash them. We may have to buy new clothes, if I can't get these clean. I'll have to scrub the floor. Hmm, my labor isn't cheap. Looks as if your bill is for more than you have in your savings accounts, unless you want to work for me on Saturday to pay this back." Needless to say, on Saturday the boys did laundry, scrubbed the floor, and did whatever else Mom asked.

This isn't the story's end, though. Mom chuckled when next day she found out they had learned their lesson. It seems that Grandma took the boys swimming, and she couldn't convince them to leave the car. It had rained again. "It was too muddy!" they said.

These examples were written with the idea that children sometimes learn from bad experiences. This was not meant, however, that we should rush them headlong into doing anything they want.

Guide Teens

Teach teens to make responsible decisions, and to handle smaller problems in a more casual way than larger ones. Finally, help them see their future not in dollars earned, but in respect earned and given.

21. Teens discover themselves

As children mature, they yearn for their own identity and try to distance themselves from their parents. They may be irresponsible, worried, scared, argumentative, and questioning. The methods some children have of identifying themselves are by unusual haircuts, messy rooms, different clothes, and the like. These situations are difficult and frustrating for parents. Make sure you understand the situation first. You might respond by using "I want," "I need," "I like" statements along with "what," "when," and "how" questions to show your loving concern. Try not to be agitated. Instead, for example, say, "I'm concerned. I would like to see you treat yourself to something fantastic, such as a clean room. I want you to be kind to yourself. How can I help?" In what positive ways would you handle a circumstance above such as haircuts, messy rooms, and so on?

_____

_____

_____

Once in awhile, we need to lighten up. Solve minor problems by a simple reverse and surprise technique. If you always react to a problem in the same old way and get the same old reaction back from your child, try responding in an opposite manner. For example, Junior comes home with fresh self-inflicted fashion holes in his brand new jeans, and your reaction the last dozen times has been, "Don't ever let me catch you tearing your pants again!" Change what you always say to something like, "The length looks right," or "I like the green shoes." Responding in a new way forces your child to think about the situation from a different and sometimes humorous angle. Consider too, the fewer words the better. Saying less gives your kids a chance to try to figure out what you are thinking. Now, try reacting to a situation above (unusual haircuts, messy rooms, etc.) with the reverse and surprise technique. Discuss minor consequences and alternatives, also. If they object, calmly and politely state something like the following:

"I hear you and I know the holes seems cool and comfortable, but I love you so much that I am going to have to insist that you present yourself better in public. You have a choice. You can fix the holes yourself, or I will help you. Do you want to do it now or at 7 p.m.? Here is a list of things that need to be done." If you still don't have a reply, state a consequence as in Exercise 4 (with a smile) such as: "Otherwise, I will do the work myself and charge you for the service."

Children need models more than they need critics.—Joseph Joubert, *Pensees*

22. Make responsible decisions

Your teenage children have a growing need for independence, but they still need guidance and understanding. Handle conflicts in a reasonable, empathic, non-judgmental, non-aggressive manner.

Example:

(a) State the problem: "We have a problem, and it is _____."

(b) Determine if these actions led or would lead to trouble.

(c) Find out their thoughts and empathize as in Exercise 4, with an "Oh" or an "Umm."

(d) Find a solution: If you still have no solution in (c) above, continue, "Something needs to be done, let's find a solution, this is not acceptable."

(e) Finally, depending on the circumstances, reconcile and talk about at least some of the following: consequences, restitution, forgiveness, compassion, and forgetting.

Your teen may have difficulty getting along at home, with a sibling, or at school with the basketball coach. Maybe your daughter's best friend is now her worst enemy. Perhaps your son doesn't understand why he can't have his body pierced or get a tattoo. Have you had an older child that rebelled? How did you handle it?

_____

_____

_____

Were you satisfied with the results?_____
If no, would the ideas (a) to (e) suggested above have helped you?_____
If yes, write down the solution for practice:

_____

_____

_____

_____

_____

23. Deal with rebellion

Rebellious teens may be distant, disrespectful, defiant, or aggressive. They need special help. Never accept verbal or physical abuse from your children. If it occurs, ask them to find a quiet place to cool down and then write their anger out on paper. Discuss the matter when they cool off. In the book, *Raising Self-Reliant Children In A Self-Indulgent World*, H. Stephen Glenn and Jane Nelsen, Ed.D. said, "Angry people cannot learn about assessing and resolving their anger. The best time to discuss an angry moment is soon enough after the incident to recall the emotion, but long enough afterward to permit objectivity."[4] Be a role model, not aggressive and hard nosed. Matching your anger with theirs only makes them angrier. Do not talk to them as if they are bad. Say, instead, the deed they did was bad.

Review (a) through (e), above, in Exercise 22 with them and help them deal with their anger. Find out if their emotional, physical, and spiritual needs are being met. Remember the prodigal son, "...he was lost and now is found" (Luke 15:32). How would you discuss your children's needs with them?

_____

_____

_____

_____

_____

Ask God for help in tough times like this. Especially, use the St. Michael prayer at the end of this book. If you still have difficulty, take parenting classes, or find help with discipline through assertiveness training courses taught in the adult education programs and community college systems across the country. These courses help you assert yourself with dignity and not with the two extremes—offense versus apprehension. The class helps you maintain your dignity, stand your ground, and stick with the facts without either getting mad or (on the contrary) conceding. In extreme cases, though, where your child shows no response, you must let go and find help through counselors, clergy, doctors, mental health clinics, and so on. Love them enough to take action. Consider this famous quote, "People need loving the most when they deserve it the least."—John Harrigan

24. Allow teens independence

We raise our children to be useful, independent, God-fearing citizens, but somehow, when they enter high school, the emphasis sometimes shifts to gaining a high-paying job. This is good to a certain extent; however, there is a Bible verse that says, "No servant can serve two masters; for either he will hate the one and love the other, or he will be devoted to the one and despise the other. You cannot serve God and mammon [money]" (Luke 16:13). How can we focus on marriage, priesthood, religious life, and single vocations when we have the complete focus on money? The answer is that we, as parents, must teach some vocation skills and faith principles ourselves. If you learn to type, you become a typist. If you learn to weld, you become a welder. Who teaches young adults, though, to become priests or other religious professionals, and parents? These are among the most important things we do in raising serious-minded, independent, faithful children; and yet, it is seldom taught. Oh Lord, help us teach our children to be the image of God.

Help young adults gain independence and fortitude to serve and protect the next generation. Together, with teenagers, write separate lists of what each of you think the words maturity and responsibility mean.

Parents' list:

_____
_____
_____
_____

Teenager's list:

_____
_____

Compare and discuss the lists. Do they include Catholic faith, family life, obedience, sacrifice, trust, self-discipline, strength, security, confidence, positive not negative influences, respecting human life, teaching, preaching, forgiveness, caring, nurturing, and providing for children? Expect varying answers from different people: Moms to Dads; girls to boys; and child to child. That's the way we were made—to complement one another.

If we put our most intense energy into providing, teaching, and nurturing the next generation, they will resound with the benefits for all eternity. One cannot say that if we teach them materialism. The next chapters give more insight on gaining responsibility and eventual independence.

In the final count, think of how Joseph and Mary would handle your child in a difficult discipline situation. Certainly, they would teach respect, firmness, and remorse, in the light of faith, hope, and love. They would take time to sit and talk about better behavior, time-outs, lost privileges, and whatever it takes to get your child to see the situation clearly.

Endnotes:

1. *Catechism of the Catholic Church* (Washington, D.C.: United States Catholic Conference, 1997), Publication no. 5-110, #2205, p. 532.

2. Gregory K., Popcak, MSW, LCSW and Lisa Popcak, *Parenting with Grace* (Huntington, Indiana: Our Sunday Visitor, 2000), pp. 350, 352, 357, 362.

3. John Rosemond, psychologist and columnist for Knight-Ridder Newspapers, "How to Motivate Children," *Grand Island (Neb.) Independent* (30 July 1993): p. 8-A.

4. Stephen Glenn and Jane Nelsen, Ed.D., *Raising Self-Reliant Children In A Self-Indulgent World* (Rocklin, CA: Prima Publishing, 1988), p. 138.

Bibliography:

American Academy of Pediatrics (AAP), for the latest in children's health and safety. Web site: www.aap.org.

Glenn, Stephen, and Jane Nelsen, Ed.D. *Raising Self-Reliant Children In A Self-Indulgent World*. California: Prima Publishing, 1988.

Popcak, Gregory, MSW, LCSW, and Lisa Popcak. *Parenting with Grace*. Indiana: Our Sunday Visitor, 2000.

Popcak, Gregory, MSW, LCSW. A Catholic psychotherapist and director of the Pastoral Solutions Institute, an organization that provides telephone counseling and referrals for Catholics struggling to apply their faith to tough marriage, family, and personal problems. Telephone: 740-266-6461, Web site: www.exceptionalmarriages.com.

Rosemond, John. *Because I Said So*. Kansas City, MO: Andrews and McMeel, 1996.

Our children's lives turn into havoc when they are not properly prepared for the storms of temptations confronting them as they enter adulthood.

Chapter III

Identify and Resist Negative Influences

The *Catechism of the Catholic Church* says, "The home is the natural environment for initiating a human being into solidarity and communal responsibilities. Parents should teach children to avoid the compromising and degrading influences which threaten human societies." [1]

Think for a moment how winter slowly sweeps into the Midwest. Farmers prepare their cattle with food and provisions for the long winter's blast. Sometimes, though, winter hits in mid-October, and the farmer hasn't had ample time to prepare; then, havoc hits the prairie. Similarly, our children's lives turn into havoc when they are not properly prepared for the storms of temptations confronting them as they enter adulthood.

Man is fallen: His intellect is darkened and his will is weakened by original sin. In man's search for restoration with God and his true self, he is buffeted by temptation and deception coming from the world, the flesh, and the devil.

Deception from the world comes from peers, media, and vainglory of ambition. In the flesh, comes pressures of the physical appetite already disordered by original sin excited and aroused by inner temptations and outside influences, such as music, books, movies, etc., that excite passions. Finally, through the devil, we have thoughts that deny or doubt God and his love for us.

So, what is the solution? Jesus. He has redeemed us by his suffering, death, and resurrection, which have broken the power of sin and death over us. We need to learn about Jesus, follow his example, and through prayer and sacraments receive his empowering grace. Children will learn to expose evil and know the truth—"he who does what is true comes to the light, that it may be clearly seen that his deeds have been wrought in God" (John 3: 21).

(Again, as you speak with your children, follow instructions from the Introduction on the suitable age for each child.)

Negative Versus Positive Peer Pressure

The first chapters dealt with positive influences and discipline. Now, you can help your adolescent children recognize and resist the storms of negative influences and show them ways to react and build positive friendships, so that they do not naively step into dangerous situations.

25. Avoid SCARE tactics

If your children know the Ten Commandments and the Corporal and Spiritual Works of Mercy, they understand that they should say no to negative peer pressure. They are seldom taught, though, to recognize those personalities who may pressure them to do bad things. There are five ways to recognize others who pressure one into this self-destructive behavior. The acronym for recognizing peer pressure is SCARE (SCARE stands for secrecy, control, addiction, ridicule, and excuses and enemies). SCARE is the first sign that an individual, organization, or even a business is trying to manipulate you. Negative peer pressure affects young and old. Adolescence, unfortunately, is the time when one is most vulnerable. This is when young people begin to question their parents' beliefs and behaviors, and start to follow the crowd.

Explain to your children the questions they must learn to ask themselves as they prepare for the occasional turbulence of negative peer pressure.

S—Secrecy—Does the other person try to conceal something from you or someone else? Is the secrecy a basis for lies and deception? Are there secrets you would rather not hear and know about this person? Have you known someone for a long time and still felt intimidated and uneasy about something he or she does?

Some people are secretive for the wrong reasons. Discuss with your children the following three examples of the dangers of secrecy. Discern whether these people deceived someone.

Examples: Trent has a new bicycle but no money. Your best friend, Trina, leaves every weekend, but never tells you where she goes. A friend tells you he never gets drunk, but has had several late-night accidents.

Response: Take one of the examples from above and ask your children to give a response such as taking time to sort through the facts, "I want to know," "I need more information," "Let's talk," "I'm concerned, what did you say?"

Prayer: Pray for people who hide the truth from you, but don't let yourself be deceived by their "disguises" (cf. 2 Corinthians 11:14).

C—Control—Does that person try to control and dominate you or others? Does he use power and control to praise some people and condemn others, thus making the condemned fearful to speak?

Positive control is sometimes good, for instance, when a teacher expects you to learn. When someone uses negative control on us, however, they have a weakness. Control is usually not wrong unless it leads to destructive behavior. Discuss with your children how the dominating people in the following instances might deceive someone.

Examples: Carl might pressure you to go to a drug party, but when you hesitate, he makes fun of you, says you are a chicken, and states that everyone else will be there but you. In another instance, Janet dates Todd. Todd dominates Janet's actions and thoughts, and seldom lets her be with other friends. Janet loves Todd, but does Todd love Janet?

Response: Take one of the examples from above and ask your children to give a good response by using persistence, tact, and patience. Here is how you might answer Carl, "I've got other plans," "Sorry, that's not my name," or "I can't be there, my ship's coming in." This could be a reply for Janet to use, "I'm puzzled about our relationship," or "I'm not following what you are trying to tell me."

Prayer: Ask God to help you know the differences between love and fear and control (cf. 1 John 4:11-21).

A—Addiction—Does the other person seem preoccupied, for instance, by money, pornography, sex, gunfire, material gain, parties, and alcohol? Has one addiction stopped and another taken its place? Does this person attempt to convince you of this obsessive lifestyle?

Addictions fill a void in our life. They satisfy a desire to be loved, respected, and honored. Yet, in the end addictions destroy us. Ask your children if they understand how the addictive people in the following instances might deceive them if this were for real.

Examples: Steve might say, "A case of beer on the weekend doesn't hurt anyone!" Susan might say, "My credit card is charged to the max. Can I borrow some money until the 15th?"

Response: Take one of the examples from above and ask your children to respond by finding alternatives, "I'm thinking this is too much. Let's talk about the outcome. I want you to find help. Let me know if you need assistance. In the meantime, let's go to my house, raid the refrigerator, and play a game of pool."

Prayer: Pray to follow our Lord's first commandment. It asks that we have "no other gods before [us]" (Exodus 20:3) including the god of addiction.

R—Ridicule—Is the other person "boastful" (Psalm 5:5), disrespectful, and rebellious against either you or someone else? Does this person "take the name of the Lord your God in vain…" (Exodus 20:7)? Are people afraid of this person for fear of put-downs and the harm this person might do? Does this person feel inferior and try to make you feel bad, also?

Ridiculing others makes us feel powerful for a short time, but soon friends catch on and start to avoid us. Ask your children if they understand how the people who ridicule in the examples below might deceive them if this were for real.

Examples: Kathy ridicules her sister by saying, "You're just afraid," when she wants her sister to swipe the family car for a few hours and cruise around town. In still another instance, Jill with her jokes and teasing might poke fun at her boyfriend, Jim. She might say, "You always wear the same old shirt."

Response: Take one of the examples from above and ask your children to give a good response by using questions such as, "Kathy, why is it so important for me to swipe the car?" or "Where are you going in such a hurry?" Jim could be direct and say, "Jill, could I ask you why it matters?" or "What's the difference?" A question not only makes the other person stop and think, but it helps you bide time and assess the situation. Keep in mind that people who scorn you have no respect for themselves or for others as well.

Prayer: Pray and look to God as your master, "Let them be put to shame and dishonor who seek after my life!…" (Psalm 35[34]: 4). Look to God for joy, kindness, love, and generosity.

E—Excuses and Enemies—Does the other person blame someone for her own faults? Does she have many excuses about why she is often on the defensive against a personal enemy?

Excuses free us from responsibility. Excuses often include lies and weaken our character, credibility, and integrity. Ask your children if they understand how the blaming people in the examples below might deceive them if this were for real.

Examples: Jane loses her assignment and tells everyone that she blames Tim who didn't take it. In another scenario, Julie breaks up with Kevin and starts dating Aaron. Kevin blames Aaron for the breakup when it was Kevin's shortcoming that caused it.

Response: Take one of the examples from above, then ask your children to give a cautious response to the accusing person. People with constantly defensive attitudes have negative feelings about their own self-worth. Therefore, try to be calm and positive. Gently explain what they do is wrong; but if they do not want help, then move away. Say something such as: "I need to go now," and "Sorry, my limo is waiting." In extreme cases, tell your child to leave the scene quickly and unobtrusively.

Prayer: Pray to help the "wrathful" (Proverbs 22:24) person. If you can't help them, though, pray to find a real friend—one that settles differences with others in a calm way that does not threaten or involve a third party such as yourself.

Explain how all people who use SCARE methods are not necessarily evil. We must, however, ask ourselves if being with them might get us into trouble. We must ask ourselves, "Am I going to follow Jesus?" and "Do these people keep me from God, family, and community?"

Ask your children to memorize the SCARE (the words: secrecy, control, addiction, ridicule, and excuses and enemies) tactics, so that they can easily recognize negative peer pressure.

Remind your children that if someone pressures them with any one of the SCARE tactics, they must remain on guard and stick up for what they believe. Tell them, though, to "...Love your enemies..." (Luke 6:27). Love the perpetrator, but not the perpetrator's SCARE procedures. Vindictive behavior from your children against him only prompts that individual to tempt your children further, and never helps that person to change his ways.

Also, remind your children that they should not dwell on negative incidents such as described here, but they should recognize these and in contrast (without being pretentious) be thankful for their own positive talents and qualities. Have children memorize the "Commandments" and "Works of Mercy" at the end of this book.

The first Spiritual Work of Mercy says to "admonish [reprove gently] sinners." Discuss with your children how each response to SCARE, above, was a gentle reprisal.

_____

26. Build positive friendships

Through the thick and thin of it all, all children need friends. As they reach adolescence, children begin to realize the importance of friendships. When children know of someone in a certain classroom or they gather with friends at a school event, it is much easier for them to make the transition from home to school or from school to school. These friends link your children with the outside world. Think about the friends you had and remember how good they made you feel. Now, think of the warmth, understanding, and communication you had with these friends. Think how your parents helped you develop friendships. Maybe your mother helped you bake cookies for a birthday party with friends, or your father helped you set up a game or two in the backyard to help attract other children from the neighborhood. How can you help your children make friends feel welcome in your home?

_____

_____

_____

_____

Children need only a couple of good friends. They need to understand that they don't have to be everyone's best friend. If they are everyone's best friend, they might be trying to please too many children and might be tempted to follow the bad element in the crowd. Children should find trust with adults and a few friends rather than develop a dependence on groups of children. If one of your children lacks in acquaintances, ask this child to think of two or three children whom you both feel would make good friends, ones who also bond well with the rest of your family, and invite them over.

We would like only to think of the good times, but a certain amount of conflict is to be expected in any relationship. If possible, parents should remain near, but uninvolved, so children learn to resolve conflicts on their own. Think of times when you, yourself, were glad that your parents refused to step in.

_____

_____

_____

_____

Getting out of your own messes most likely helped you develop a responsible attitude. Allow your children to be accountable for their friendly and not-so-friendly relationships up to a certain point. However, keep the lines of communication open with children; they need your love and concern. If it sounds too dangerous for them to handle alone, or if their emotions cause them to break down, then of course you must step in and help.

Recall a difficult peer pressure situation that may have happened to your child and write it below. (If you have none, make one up, such as teasing and blaming, or use a newspaper or magazine clipping, for example, on drugs, alcohol, sexual abuse, violence, or persecution of faith.)

_____
_____
_____
_____

Did any of the five SCARE characteristics pertain to the above incident? Make notes below with your child.

Secrecy
_____
_____

Control
_____
_____

Addiction
_____
_____

Ridicule
_____
_____

Excuses/Enemies
_____
_____

Again, as shown in Exercise 25, under responses, these are a few ways to deal with the SCARE situations:

* Take time to sort through the facts.
* Respond with patience, persistence, and tact.
* Find alternatives.
* Ask questions.
* Use caution.

Together, write down at least one of the ideas that was used, or could have been used, to counteract the SCARE situations you listed. Explain that if the incident could not be resolved and it was against their moral conviction, you would expect them to walk away.

_____

_____

_____

_____

Perchance it went like this: Your teen comes home from school in a bad mood. He had a conflict with a friend. The "friend" called him a name and your child hit him, knocked him down, and was ordered by the teacher to stay after school. Tell your child there are better ways than fighting to solve a conflict. Tell your child to respond with a positive, "I want," "I expect," "I need," "I like," or "fact" statement. With patience and persistence, say, for instance, "I need to be called something better, thanks," or make a joke of it, act silly and say "What did you say?...Yaw, sure." Tell your child that the less he says the better, and that this will gain him respect from onlookers as well.

Note to children: Those who pressure and harass you try to find someone to do things as badly as they have done. If they can get someone else to practice similar bad behavior, it gives them an "okay" to continue their style of living. At times, you can deflect them with humor and grace; however, if they won't listen to you and won't stop pressuring you, then be cautious, say "no thanks," and ignore them or leave. Fighting (except in extreme life or death cases) and name-calling are never good alternatives. Combat only makes them angry and they may never leave you alone. If you feel the need for your parents or another adult such as a teacher to intervene, ask them to do so.

Ultimately, pray for perpetrators of evil deeds. Feel sorry for them. They may not know of a charitable way to act. They may have no knowledge of the goodness and self-control demonstrated in the Eight Beatitudes. Read and memorize the Beatitudes in the back of the book. See how these declarations are in direct opposition to the SCARE tactics of secrecy, control, addiction, ridicule, and excuses and enemies. Forgive with an "It's okay," and have courage enough to ask forgiveness and to negotiate if you had a part in the escalation of a conflict. God would want you to leave your resentments behind.

Jesus reminds us in the Beatitudes, "the meek...shall inherit the earth," and "the peacemakers...shall be called sons of God" (Matthew 5:5,9).

Negative Versus Positive Entertainment

Just as advertisements entice us to buy their products, so do industries entice us to entertain ourselves with their morality or immorality. We can entertain ourselves in many beneficial ways, but we must learn to discern good from bad.

27. Form criteria

Our basic right to freedom of speech is good. It is damaging, though, when children can hear (and see) every violent and sexual scenario in the media. Parents should not allow children to listen to and watch the thousands of immoral encounters on television each year. *The Splendor of Truth* says this about immorality, "From the theological viewpoint, moral principles are not dependent upon the historical moment in which they are discovered."[2] Too often, though, we hear that morals come from our customs and, therefore, we assume anything in our culture is all right. This is wrong. Christian morals come from the very word of God.

Children learn many secular ideas from television. Although a few programs are wholesome, some psychologists recommend no more than 0-6 hours per week of television viewing for children under eight years of age. Psychologist Jane Healy, author *of Endangered Minds: Why Children Don't Think*, said "research strongly indicates that it [television and other forms of video] has the potential to [adversely] affect both the brain itself and related learning abilities."[3] Time away from television gives children a chance to develop not only their morals, but also their intellectual, social, creative, and physical being. Dare to turn it off and read, play, build, pray. If you watch it, view it together—even cartoons!

Teach morality to your children a little at a time until they fully comprehend Catholic teaching. One method of doing this would be to make comments about poor media programming. The softer you whisper your concerns, the better young people overhear you! On the contrary, saying nothing condones the content of material watched or heard, and saying too much, too loud, turns children off. Apathy speaks as loudly as negativity.

How can you tell your children that offensive, harmful television programs (movies, Internet, games, rock music, books, and magazines, too) are not the places to learn about morality and sexual relationships, and watching or listening may be sinful or near occasions of sin?

_____

_____

_____

28. Set guidelines

Not only do corrupt entertainments offend Jesus, but also immoral pastimes affect us. Our goal is to serve the Lord, not Hollywood idols. Listed below are some ways to know whether a particular entertainment is moral. With your child, discuss a form of entertainment (particular movie, television or radio program, Web site, book, magazine, CD, tapes, or video game, for instance) that you both observed lately and see if you can answer yes to the following:

Did it support your faith in the Lord and make you more certain of your Christianity?

Did it uphold family and make life better and encourage you to associate with Mom, Dad, or siblings?

Did it champion chastity and not impurity?

Did it make you feel God-empowered and not self-empowered?

Did it entice you to be strong and holy, not weak and irreligious?

Was it moral and not "relatively" moral?

Did it, with the grace of God, transform you from sin and not transform the sin?

Did it improve your talents and not make you less gifted?

Did it make you more prayerful and not less inclined to devotion?

Did it make you more eager to learn and not lazy and less enthused about faith, work, or studies?

If you answered no to any of the above, explain where you stand on this entertainment.

_____

_____

_____

_____

How would you explain to your children that you want to scan the books, magazines, videos, CD's and tapes they bring home? Also, discuss your views on certain movies, television programs, arcade games, and Web sites. Talk about how long they can watch or play depending on content, day of week, time of day, age of child, and the necessity of your presence.

_____

_____

_____

_____

29. Provide enriching alternatives

It is easy to set passive children in front of a television screen or computer game to indulge them. It is, though, more gratifying to them if they learn how to mingle with others or entertain themselves at times. They might play board games; go biking or skating; learn a new skill such as woodworking, cooking, or sewing; play running games; make crafts; paint pictures; play with toys; invite a friend to play; decorate their room; make holiday decorations; and so forth. Ask your children about their preferences.

_____

_____

_____

_____

Children learn from hands-on activities. This is what prepares them to mature. Electronics may be a necessity in a future job, however, there is much more to life than sitting in front of a monitor.

Find Jesus

If we follow the life of Jesus, we do not have to fear temptation, because Christ triumphed over evil and we can too. God gives us grace to endure. With prayer, sacraments, and commitment, we find the strength to overcome difficulty.

30. Understand Peace

Jesus came into the world to bring peace. Tom, a soon-to-be-ordained priest, attended a service in Manger Square in Bethlehem and said this in his newsletter:

> I will share with you one grace I received on Christmas Eve in Bethlehem….During the German Sermon, which was preceded by the Arabic Sermon, I stepped outside on a veranda for a few moments as I waited for the English sermon….As I looked over the town of Bethlehem, I could see the Palestinian Authority police in the streets. I could see people going into shops. One man was closing his shop, sweeping the floor and locking the doors. Some boys down the street were arguing and yelling. Some people set off some loud fireworks, causing some people in the church to wonder if we were under attack. I saw some Christmas tree lights in a window far off in the distance. It was a very regular night, and then it came to me. On the night Jesus

was born, people were going about their lives in the usual way. Into this, this humanity, Jesus came. Sometimes we want to protect Jesus from the reality of our humanity, but he did not protect himself. At the same time, I wondered, is this a special night for me, or am I going about my usual routine? I do not think that these words communicate all of what I experienced in those few minutes looking over the city of our Lord's birth, but I hope they give you some insight into what I experienced. There are many who are working against peace. Let us pray that peace prevails.[4]

That night in Bethlehem, Tom "saw" Jesus in a real, human way. The baby Jesus was God, the Supreme Being of the whole universe, but he was a man, too. He came into the world to reconcile everyone to the Father. That is the meaning of peace.

Read Tom's story with your children. How would you help them understand that Christ triumphed over evil in this world, and gave us grace and blessings to overcome trial?

_____

_____

_____

_____

31. Seek strength in rosary and other prayer

God gives peace, strength, joy, and truth to all people, especially those in trial, as illustrated through the Mysteries of the Rosary:

Joyful Mysteries

* The "Joyful Mysteries" of the Rosary tell us how Jesus began his existence on this earth.

First, The Annunciation: The angel asked Mary to be the mother of God. Mary said yes to God, although she was not yet married to Joseph. (cf. Luke 1:26-38)

Second, The Visitation: Mary was pregnant with Jesus. She traveled a long distance to help Elizabeth and her new baby, John the Baptist. She said to Mary, '..."Blessed are you among women, and blessed is the fruit of your womb!"' (Luke 1:42).

Third, The Birth of Jesus: Jesus was born in a stable "because there was no place for them in the inn." (Luke 2:7). Later they fled to Egypt because Herod wanted to kill Jesus (cf. Matthew 2:13-14).

Fourth, The Presentation: Mary and Joseph presented Jesus at the temple where Simon greeted them. He said, '…"Behold, this child is set for the fall and rising of many in Israel, and for a sign that is spoken against (and a sword will pierce through your own soul also), that thoughts out of many hearts may be revealed"' (Luke 2:34).

Fifth, Finding in the Temple: Joseph and Mary found Jesus after he was lost (cf. Luke 2:41-52).

Reflection: Relate to your children that God gave his people peace and goodness even in times of trial.

Sorrowful Mysteries

* The "Sorrowful Mysteries" of the Rosary tell of the last days of Jesus' life on Earth. Jesus had a tough mission to fulfill, as we all do.

First, Agony in the Garden: A "distressed" Jesus asked the Father "if it were possible, the hour might pass from him" (Mark 14:33,35).

Second, Scourging at the Pillar: The cruel soldiers "scourged" our Lord (Mark 15:15).

Third, Crowning with Thorns: The soldiers crowned our Lord with "thorns…mocked him…" and "led him away…" (Matthew 27:29-31). Jesus, though, knew his kingdom wasn't of this world.

Fourth, Carrying of the Cross: Our Lord carried the cross to "Gol'gotha" (John 19:17).

Fifth, The Crucifixion: The soldiers nailed him to the cross and he forgave them (cf. Luke 23:33-34).

Reflection: Discuss the strength Christ showed us on his journey to the cross.

Glorious Mysteries

* The "Glorious Mysteries" of the Rosary describe joy as Jesus rose from the dead and brought us new life.

First, The Resurrection: Jesus rose from the dead (cf. Mark 16:6).

Second, The Ascension: Jesus ascended into heaven (cf. Mark 16:19).

Third, The Descent of the Holy Spirit: The Holy Spirit descended in "tongues as of fire…" (Acts 2:3).

Fourth, The Assumption of the Blessed Virgin Mary: Mary was taken up to Heaven and was united with Jesus.

Fifth, The Crowning of the Blessed Virgin Mary: Scripture has it, "on her head a crown of twelve stars" (Revelation 12:1).

Reflection: Discuss the happiness Jesus gives to those who follow his path and believe in him.

Luminous Mysteries

* The "Luminous Mysteries" of the Rosary describe to us the truths of his public life.

First, Baptism of Jesus in the Jordan: John the Baptist baptized Jesus (cf. Matthew 3:13).

Second, Jesus' Self-manifestation at the Wedding of Cana: This was Jesus' first miracle (cf. John 2:11)

Third, Proclamation of the Kingdom of God with His Call to Conversion: He calls us to spirituality. (cf. Mark 1:14-15).

Fourth, The Transfiguration: Jesus took Peter, James, and John to a mountain "and he was transfigured before them, and his garments became glistening…" (Mark 9:2,3).

Fifth, The Last Supper and the Institution of the Eucharist: The Eucharist is the sacramental expression of the Easter mystery (cf. I Corinthians 11:26).

Reflection: Discuss the truth Jesus gave us, considering that many people were already set in their ways and did not believe him.

When we have problems, we can dwell on the dignity and courage Jesus demonstrated in his life, especially in his teachings, and in his sufferings on the way to the cross, "through many tribulations we must enter the kingdom of God" (Acts 14:22).

Discuss true peace, strength, happiness, and truth as you recite a decade of the rosary together: one "Our Father," ten "Hail Mary's," and one "Glory Be." Mary, Queen of the Rosary, said this to St. Dominic and Blessed Alan.

[Honoring Jesus through] The rosary will make virtue and good works flourish, and will obtain for souls the most abundant divine mercies; it will substitute in hearts love of God for love of the world, elevate them to desire heavenly and eternal goods. Oh, that souls would sanctify themselves by this means![5]

Finally, explain the beauty of the complete rosary: It begins with the "Apostles' Creed," one "Our Father," and three "Hail Mary's," followed by five decades, and ends with the prayer, "Hail, Holy Queen."

Continue to use all the prayers at the back of the book with your children. A special one is the "Act of Contrition." First, ask them to examine their conscience and see what they have done wrong, and have them decide what they could have done better. Then, together, pray and review the importance of the words, "I dread the loss of heaven." Say it with them before bedtime each night along with the "Evening Prayer" and other prayers until they have each one memorized.

How would you emphasize to your children not only to pray after a bad time comes, but also to pray for prevention of it? Then, praise God and thank him for the good times.

---

32. Embrace sacramental life

Do your children understand the Lord's Prayer, or on the other hand, do they know it so well that they sail right through it and don't understand what it means? When it comes to "forgive us our trespasses as we forgive those who trespass against us," do they understand how important it is to forgive others and not hold grudges? Do they understand that our Lord asks us to be forgiving people? The Sacraments of Reconciliation and Holy Communion help us to be better people. Jesus forgives our worst sins in Reconciliation and comes to us in the Eucharist. The Eucharist is no longer bread and wine. It is the body and blood of our Lord. How would you stress to your children that Jesus redeems us and wants us to confess our sins when needed, and utilize the Eucharist often, on Sundays and holy days, and even daily for the forgiveness of sins and the good of the world?

Jesus came into a not-so-perfect world to save us. We can show our Lord that we accept his blessings by honoring him in the sacraments.

There are five other sacraments besides Reconciliation and the Eucharist: Baptism, Confirmation, Anointing of the Sick, Holy Orders, and Matrimony.

They are central to our religion, instituted by Christ to give grace. Our happiness comes from being joined to the Lord, and we can do that by relating to Jesus in the sacraments. You grow when you encounter and come together with Christ, just as you grow with a friend. There is a difference, though, in the sacraments, Jesus empowers us to do Godly things.

33. Gain courage

Bishop Fulton J. Sheen observed "who" would effectively manage negative peer pressure. He said:

> [R]ebirth of youth will come from youth itself. If the legal profession ever became corrupt, it would not be bettered by doctors giving them lectures, but by honest lawyers regenerating their profession from within. So it is with youth. Social workers, courts, and even the clergy will only be the indirect agents for remaking a creative youth. As the Communists [They and others are a sad threat in this age, too.] lay hold of a few corrupt individuals to corrupt the mass, the leaders of youth will find among them a vast army who are specially competent in the way of leadership, who refuse to bend the knee to false gods, and who will take away the reservations from the punks and give it to the young who will be "squares" like Lincoln, Washington and other great Americans.[6]

Again, remind your children that they will face negative peer pressure, but Christ, too, had crosses to bear. From Bishop Sheen's writing, how would you ask your children to make courageous decisions based not on false gods but rather on Christ and Christian leaders?

_____

_____

_____

_____

Courage is almost a contradiction in terms. It means a strong desire to live taking the form of a readiness to die.—G. K. Chesterton, *Orthodoxy*

Now, with the first three chapters in mind on love and respect, discipline, and peer pressure, go forward. According to directions for the age groups suggested in the introductions, talk to your children about the adverse effects of drugs, sexual abuse, and violence.

Endnotes:

1. *Catechism of the Catholic Church* (Washington, D.C.: United States Catholic Conference, 1997), Publication no. 5-110, #2224, p. 537.

2. John Paul II, *The Splendor of Truth* (Boston: St. Paul Books and Media, 1999), p. 135.

3. Jane Healy, psychologist, *Endangered Minds: Why Our Children Don't Think,* (New York: Simon and Shuster, 1991), p. 216.

4. Thomas Simonds, S.J., newsletter, 19 Jan. 1997, Pine Ridge, South Dakota.

5. From the writings of Blessed Alan de Rupe.

6. Bishop Fulton J. Sheen, *Walk With God* (New York: Maco Magazine Corporation, 1965), p. 38.

Bibliography:

Catholic Families Network, provides filtered Internet Access so you and your children can enjoy all the Web has to offer in truly catholic experience. Telephone: 1-800-707-5279, Web site: www.catholicfamilies.net.

Games for Catholic Families, 28 different Church approved games based on the new Catechism and the Bible. Telephone: 1-800-669-9200, Web site: www.catholicgames.com.

Fox, Rev. Robert J., ed. *Immaculate Heart Messenger* magazine, Waite Park, MN 56287-0515: Fatima Family Apostolate, P.O. Box 515, Telephone: 1-800-721-MARY.

Healy, Jane psychologist. *Endangered Minds: Why Our Children Don't Think.* New York: Simon and Shuster, 1991.

Montfort, Saint Louis De. *The Secret of the Rosary.* Bay Shore, NY: Montfort Publications, 1999.

Parent Television Council. *PTC Insider* magazine. Burbank, CA: P.O. Box 7802, Web site: www.parentstv.org.

Use time-tested methods to prevent your children from drowning in drugs and other addictions.

Chapter IV

Discuss Substance Abuse

"Woe to those who rise early in the morning, that they may run after strong drink, who tarry late into the evening till wine inflames them! They have lyre and harp, timbrel and flute and wine at their feasts; but they do not regard the deeds of the Lord, or see the work of his hands" (Isaiah 5:11-12).

Whether or not teen (and adult) usage of drugs and alcohol and other abusive substances increases or decreases, rates are consistently more than they should be. What method can you use to teach your children not to drown in the pools of drugs and other addictions? Think as the experts. Take, for example, the methods taught by a swimming coach. Foremost, the coach is well qualified and uses superb techniques. Then he communicates the procedures of safe conduct. Lastly, he helps his students predict the results of playing in unsafe river holes.

Likewise, use these time-tested methods to prevent your children from drowning in drugs and other addictions. In this chapter, first, you learn the qualifications of an instructor and use the highest expectations of faith and good example. Second, you teach your children how to understand safety from drugs and other abuses. Finally, you teach your children the consequences of swimming in the river holes of intoxication.

In this way, children learn facts, gain responsibility, and exercise caution about chemical dangers. Still they enjoy their social lives. Satisfying pastimes do not have to mean all-night hangovers, or worse.

The *Catechism of the Catholic Church* says of temperance:

> The virtue of temperance disposes us to *avoid every kind of excess*: the abuse of food, alcohol, tobacco, or medicine. Those incur grave

guilt who, by drunkenness or a love of speed, endanger their own and others' safety on the road, at sea, or in the air.

The *use of drugs* inflicts very grave damage on human health and life. Their use, except on strictly therapeutic grounds, is a grave offense. Clandestine production of and trafficking in drugs are scandalous practices. They constitute direct co-operation in evil, since they encourage people to practices gravely contrary to the moral law.[1]

(Again, as you proceed with speaking to your children, follow instructions from the Introduction for the ages of each child.)

Substance Abuse and Prevention

Would kids in a swim class know how to make wise decisions in a dangerous predicament if the instructor didn't promote safety? Then, why do we, as parents, think we can turn kids loose on Saturday night without instructions, and believe they won't touch a drop of alcohol or other drugs? What makes us think that silence is deterrence? Teach adolescents about the harmful and addictive effects of alcohol and other drugs. Teach them to avoid alcohol and drugs, and the drug pushers, and their harmful substances. Set good examples and give children alternatives.

34. Learn facts about alcohol

Moderation of alcohol and a few other substances is like moderation of guns. When used properly, guns put food on our table and protect us, but when used wrongly, they become deadly and we commit serious crime. Adults who sip wine at a dinner table and use it at the Eucharist may not pose a threat to their health, except if they are alcoholics. A glass of beer on a hot day for most adults is fine, but excessive alcohol has serious effects on our bodies and souls.

A difference exists between alcohol and other chemicals. Alcohol is produced through the fermentation of fruits and grains. Some alcoholic beverages, therefore, actually have healthful attributes and can enhance or aid in the digestion of food. However, excessive amounts of alcohol produce harmful effects, and for those with no tolerance of alcohol, any amount can result in harm. One of the harmful effects of over-consumption of alcohol is intoxication, in which people lose control over their physical and mental faculties. It is always a sin to become intoxicated! Alcohol, though, can be consumed without intoxication. On the other hand, many chemicals are available today that are only consumed for the intoxicating effects! That is why it is illegal and wrong to partake of these in any amount!

Children understand logic by the age of twelve. What age do you want your children to be when you begin to speak to them about the spiritual and physical problems of drugs and alcohol? _____

Share a drug or alcohol tragedy that happened in your lifetime.

_____

_____

_____

_____

One gains freedom by doing the right thing, but slavery comes from using abusive substances such as marijuana, crack cocaine, and methamphetamines that alter your mind and body. Addiction to drugs and alcohol equals allegiance to a false God. How would you explain to your children that addiction violates the first commandment, "I am the Lord thy God. Thou shalt not have strange Gods before me"?

_____

_____

_____

_____

From the beginning of this chapter, read Bible and Catechism passages to your children.

35. Learn effects of addictions

Children do not understand how things either common or uncommon in everyday life result in addiction. Children need to also understand that various people have different metabolisms. That is, what has little or no effect on one person may have serious effects on another. Sometimes these addictive behaviors lead to still other addictions. When you teach your children, be careful not to arouse their curiosity, especially about substances such as inhalants, over-the-counter-drugs, and others that could lead to experimentation. The following are a few of the health and social problems associated with addictive behaviors that you might want to share with your children:

Caffeine: Caffeine, if used in excess, causes loss of sleep and restricts blood vessels.

Eating Disorders: A bulimic person has an insatiable desire for food but purges it. Anorexics, on the other hand, lose their appetite. These are diseases or psychological disorders. Those addicted usually want a thin body. It can lead to death.

Gambling: Gamblers become addicted to the thrill of betting large sums of money. This damaging psychological addiction often interferes with family life, leaves people in poverty, and involves forms of chemical addiction. A 1999 (compared to 1975) report said, "the ratio of adults who have never gambled has dropped from roughly one out of three to one out of seven, and gambling expenditures have increased from 0.30 percent…to 0.74 percent of personal income."[2]

Inhalants (such as, hair spray, nail polish remover, spray paint, paint thinner, gasoline, magic marker, air freshener, oven spray, furniture polish and wax, correction fluid, glue, drain cleaner, ammonia, cooking spray, moth balls, and butane): These cause nausea, depression, violence, suicide, dizzy spells, loss of memory, and hallucinations. The Alcohol and Drug Information Clearinghouse said, "Some chemicals damage nerve endings, or the brain itself. Some cause heart attacks, and others are linked to cancer, or to liver or kidney damage. Some cause breathing problems, and some cause sudden death."[3] Some warning signs are sores on the mouth, gold and silver paint stains, and chemical odors.

Prescription and Over-the-Counter Drugs: Some forms of legal drugs cause addiction. They also may be life threatening when used in excess and in combination with other drugs. Read all instructions with every drug and follow your doctor's advice.

Television Watching, Computer Games, Workaholism, Speeding, and Consumerism: These pastimes are physiologically addictive when they interfere with school, work, health, relationships, and ability to be well-rounded Christians.

(Whereas eating disorders, gambling, and some pastimes above are not potions in themselves, these form a chemical component in the body similar to drugs. This is the reason they are so difficult to overcome.)

Authorities recognize teenage tobacco, alcohol, and marijuana use (below), as signs of vulnerability to peer pressure and as a gateway to other drugs. It would be good to discuss in detail the harm of these with your children because these are so common. On the other hand, it may be to your advantage to recognize the other drugs, but not tell everything to children. Here is an example of what could happen: A sixth-grade student attended a citywide anti-drug program. The people in charge described the name, properties, use, and so forth of drugs. When the child came home, he related to his mother, "They told me and my friends how to do drugs!" Explain the dangers, but not every detail. If your child, though, has questions and you need more information, one excellent book that describes drugs is *Growing Up Drug Free* listed in the bibliography.

Some information that you as a parent may need to know is the following:

Tobacco: Tobacco, according to the United States Department of Education, causes: addiction; "cancer of the lung, larynx, esophagus, bladder, pancreas, kidney, and mouth"; "emphysema and chronic bronchitis"; and "spontaneous abortion, pre-term delivery, and low birth weight."[4]

Alcohol: It causes anything from changes in behavior, judgment, and coordination to aggression, mental impairment, dependence, brain and liver damage, birth defects, and death. Knowledge and respect for one's limits requires maturity. The reason the law forbids sale of alcohol to people under twenty-one is the widespread lack of maturity below that age. This irresponsible consumption follows with reckless behavior that endangers the lives and property of you and others.

Cannabis (marijuana, Tetrahydrocannabinol (THC), hashish): Some of its effects are problems with short-term memory, concentration, heart rate, paranoia, hallucinations, behavior, and motivation.[5]

Cocaine: Immediate effects may be dilated pupils, increased heart rate, and a stuffy nose. The book, *Getting it Straight*, by the Justice Department, concludes, "they are usually depressed, edgy, and craving for more. First time users can experience seizures or heart attacks which can be fatal."[6]

Methamphetamines (speed, meth, crank, crystal): It causes "anxiety, increased blood pressure, paranoia/psychosis, aggression, nervousness, hypothermia, compulsive behavior, stroke, depression, convulsions...hallucinations...arrhythmia" and more.[7]

LSD (lysergic acid diethylamides): This mood-altering drug affects the way you perceive things such as time, sound, color, direction, and distance. Some have feelings of "depression, anxiety, fear, and panic." Some have behavior that makes you think you can fly off of buildings or walk in front of cars without getting hurt.[8]

When we spend time on addictive behavior, we tend to forget God's plan for us.

At what age did you learn about these addictions?_____

At what age do you want your children to be when you discuss the above addictions with them?_____

Children have many advantages if they recognize the dangers of overuse and abuse, just as swimmers need to know about quicksand in a river hole. Explain how these addictions affect them, their families, their spiritual life, and their community. Also, explain your expectations about those dangers.

_____
_____
_____
_____

How would you explain that exuberance comes with freedom from, and not bondage to, chemicals that take over and ruin our lives, and even land us in jail or in poverty and on the street?

_____
_____
_____
_____

36. Acquire the virtue of temperance

Substance abuse prevention begins with good examples and instruction from parents. Temperance is a cardinal virtue. God expects us to cultivate this virtue. Anything short of a virtuous life hurts us physically and spiritually. How many of the listed family and community ideas can you implement to help your children (and your grandchildren) stay clear of drugs and alcohol?

* Exercise the virtue of temperance yourself. Limit alcohol in your home to small quantities and keep it locked away. If an alcoholic dwells within your family, then there should be no alcohol at all in the home.

* Take a stand against alcohol and drug abuse, and work with parent organizations to bring anti-abuse material to the schools. The local police force is usually more than willing to help.

* Show your children that members of your family can overcome stress without having to "escape" from their emotions with drugs or alcohol. Show them that exercise, relaxation, conversation, outdoor recreation, and prayer relieve stress. If they need more encouragement, seek counseling to alleviate family stress. Help your children realize they aren't the only ones who have problems.

* The book, *Growing up Drug Free* said children choose drugs to "…have fun…take risks, ease their pain, feel grown-up, show their independence, belong to a specific group, [and] look cool."[9] Therefore, conduct parent-and community-sponsored events for children that allow them to have fun and build relationships without drugs and alcohol.

* Turn adult cocktail parties, receptions, and New Year celebrations into Coke tale parties, or at least set alcohol limits. Have plenty of non-alcoholic drinks available. Explain to your children why you set limits.

* Keep in close contact with other parents, especially when your children visit their homes, because many keg parties are conducted at home when parents are present!

* Be at home when children need you the most. *The Harvard Medical School Mental Health Letter* said:

> The first weeks and months of a child's life are a sensitive period for emotional development, and the quality of later childhood and adult relationships often reflects the relationship with caregivers established during this time.…Research shows that this foundation is important for a child's social, emotional, and cognitive development. Children without it lack self-esteem, make few friends, mistrust adults, and develop behavior problems.[10]

Another authority suggested that you should not leave your *teen* alone. They showed a direct correlation between the amount of time teens were without their parents and the amount they abused drugs and alcohol. Try to be home with your children through the teen years, too. Never miss an opportunity for hugs or pats on the shoulder. Children may be lonelier than we think.

Children need parental or other adult supervision (especially through Church sources). Children who don't find security in the home or with some kindly adult follow anyone in the crowd who shows them a little friendship because they, themselves, are starved for it. Nevertheless, the respect one gives to children when they are young is the respect one gets back when they are eighteen and twenty-four, and beyond.

* Begin now to evaluate the high schools and colleges that your children might attend. Find out if and how the school discourages drug and alcohol consumption.

Teach your children self-control in all areas of their lives (refer to self-denial in Exercise 2). Explain how you can make a difference in the items above.

_____

_____

_____

37. Teaching moments

Counsel your children about the risks of substance abuse in two steps. First, find out their views about the risks so that you discuss the facts from both sides of the question—theirs and yours. Then, tell them your expectations. Avoid threats. The best way to get your children to do something is to angrily tell them *not* to do it! Ironic as that might sound, a threatening "don't" is interpreted as "do" in a child's mind. Also, avoid hasty judgments, critical remarks, and pretentious attitudes. Teaching should come not in long complex lectures, but in short moments throughout their teenage years. Some examples for teaching about risks and your expectations against those risks follow:

* Communicate to your children the **physical, mental, and spiritual side effects** of drugs and alcohol.

Example: "Mark, do you know about the physical, mental, and spiritual effects of drugs and alcohol?"…Find out what he knows and then say (if he does not already know) something like the following: "The long-term physical and mental effects of drugs and alcohol are addiction and death. Short-term effects include headaches, vomiting, dizziness, reduced motivation, deteriorating family relationships, aggressiveness, and mental deterioration. First and foremost, however, the spiritual side effect is that it is a sin and offends God." Then give your expectation, "I hope our family avoids substance abuse." (More effects are back in Exercise 35.)

Now, use your own words to express concerns.

_____

_____

_____

_____

* Communicate to your children the **false sense of security** one gets from the use of drugs and alcohol.

Example: "Keri, do you know that alcohol and drugs become a social way of life for some?"...Find out her opinion and then say (if she does not already know) something like the following: "Some insecure people find it hard to socialize without a glass of beer in their hand. Such reliance, though, on intoxicating beverages can result in addiction. I hope you find other ways to be sociable."

Now, use your own words to express concerns.

_____

_____

_____

_____

* Communicate to your children **the risks of using drugs and alcohol for celebrating**.

Example: "Jon, did you know alcohol consumption is illegal for people under twenty-one?"...Find out what he knows and then say (if he does not already know) something like the following: "Here's why; people under that age are more likely to overindulge and run into problems of unsafe driving, crime, and so forth. I expect you to celebrate with your friends by having non-alcoholic beverages, mountains of food, and plenty of activities scheduled."

Now, use your own words to express concerns.

_____

_____

_____

_____

* Communicate to your children the **risks of using drugs and alcohol to boost one's ego**.

Example: "Jeremy, some people use alcohol and drugs as a crutch to resolve their problems—do you believe that would be a good way to solve problems?"...Then say (if he does not already know) something like the following: "Rather than mend problems, alcohol and drugs help you lose control of problems. A better way to clear up difficulties is to find parents, friends, and counselors to talk about solutions."

Now, use your own words to express concerns.

_____

_____

_____

_____

* Communicate to your children **the danger of high-risk substances**.

Example: "Ashley, did you know that some drugs are stronger now than they were a few years ago, and some people are more at risk than others?"…Discuss this statement on drugs from the Department of Education:

> The high potency of marijuana on the market today makes it more dangerous than ever. THC, a psychoactive ingredient in marijuana, is fat-soluble, and its accumulation in the body has many adverse biological effects. Cocaine is one of the most addictive drugs known and sometimes causes death. It takes less alcohol to produce impairment in youth than in adults.[11]

Tell them something like the following: "These facts frighten me. One young girl thought she enjoyed her first puffs of marijuana, but found that getting 'high' required increasing amounts of the substance. She became tolerant of the drug and needed more and more to get high. At the end, she cared about nothing but where she would get her next hit. Do you have any questions?"

Now, use your own words to express concerns.

_____

_____

_____

_____

38. SCARE and substance abuse

Exercise 25 discusses peer pressure and gives precautions against it. With the help of the acronym SCARE from these pages, learn to ask your children problem solving questions about addictions. For instance, you could ask your children some of the following questions to open further communication about alcohol, drugs, and the abusers:

S—SECRECY—What do you think is the reason so many people hide the fact they are either selling or using drugs? What do you think are the reasons most parents don't know about drug parties? When you become a parent, would you want to know what your child is doing? Would it be possible that "friends" you always trusted could pressure you to do drugs? When confronted with their behavior, why do addicts deny they are chemically dependent?

C—CONTROL—Do you think drugs are in control of the person, or do you think the person is in control of the drugs? Could a person who tries to control you with alcohol and drugs, as in Proverbs 20:1, cause you physical or spiritual harm? How do drug and alcohol abusers try to manipulate others? How do tobacco and beer ads lure young people into substance abuse? How do you suppose a television, computer, or peers could control your life?

A—ADDICTION—What percentage of eighth graders do you think abuse alcohol? (Answer: According to the United States Department of Education, "25% of eighth graders have admitted to being intoxicated at least once."[12]) What gigantic problems do you think heavy drinkers have, whether or not they are eighth graders? M. David Meagher, head of a nationwide training and consulting organization on addiction said: "...the beginning of loss of control [is]...He does not get drunk every time he drinks, but he is no longer certain what will happen once he starts using alcohol. Some days he can control the use, while on others he can't. This will also happen with drugs other than alcohol."[13] Is substance abuse ever worth the harm it causes? One woman said she couldn't quit after her first try of methamphetamine. Do you believe that could happen? Do you think that people addicted to caffeine, eating disorders, gambling, inhalants, over-the-counter drugs, television, and tobacco ever thought they would become hooked on them?

R—RIDICULE—Do you think others would ridicule you for not using drugs? Do you think others would put you down so they could look better than you do? Do you think they would mock you into conforming so they would not feel guilty about their own consumption? Would these people be reliable friends if they teased you, ostracized you, or embarrassed you? Why do you think some people would want to ridicule others for not using drugs?

E—EXCUSES and ENEMIES—Have you ever heard anyone make flagrant excuses and blame others for his (the abuser's) faults? Do you think that drug pushers would make excuses about why they made enemies with nonusers? You become like those you hang out with. Do you think this is the case when you associate with those who do drugs?

Teenagers need to recognize these traits in their peers, and to know how to remain on somewhat neighborly terms with them. Entirely turning on them only creates ill will. Also, the perpetrator finds others to support him in the drinking habit, and the non-drinker, afraid of losing all his friends, begins to want to drink so that he fits back in with the crowd. Help your children remain civil toward others, but let them know you will not allow them to become close friends with those continuing to abuse drugs or alcohol. The time to break away from questionable company is when one's involvement would place one in harms way. How would you explain to your children when to cut off a harmful relationship?

_____

_____

_____

_____

What rules and consequences for breaking them, will you enforce to keep your children away from harmful substances?

_____

_____

_____

_____

Go back to "responses" in Exercises 25 and 26. Discuss ways to say "no" to a roommate who wants to have a beer party at your apartment, or to a friend who invites you to an all-night party on the river, or to someone who treats you badly because you drink soda instead of liquor. Discuss how you can say "yes" to your own alcohol-free and drug-free parties. The ultimate questions are the following: "Am I going to be controlled by peers? Am I going to be addicted to persons, places, and things? Am I going to be ridiculed by evil? Am I going to give in to enemies and their excuses? Or am I going to follow Jesus?"

Sirach 18:30 speaks of self-control, "Do not follow your base desires but restrain your appetites." Share with your children how you would want them to control their desires.

_____

_____

_____

_____

Those who use an abusive substance misuse their body and soul, and yet much peer pressure abounds for them to try it. Let your children know that they should not go to a party with alcohol and drugs no matter how tempting. Let them know if the condition arises, you will help them find new friends and new pastimes.

39. Set example at home

Families suffer abuse from either the alcohol or drug addict that lives within their household. Furthermore, victims too often cover up for the addict, and they enable more abuse to continue. The cases of those who would say, "He loves to have fun when he's high," and "She only drinks too much on special occasions," and "He needs something for relaxation" have lived to regret those words. Years later, the abuse, death, addiction, and broken relationships raise their ugly heads.

If addiction is a problem in your home, how can you show your children your disapproval of the abuser's reliance on these substances?

_____

_____

_____

_____

How can you encourage the addict to get help? (More information is ahead in Exercise 42 of this chapter.)

_____

_____

_____

_____

If you believe you are married to an alcoholic or drug addict, check the SCARE acronym and apply it to your circumstances. Ask yourself, "Do I truly care enough about my spouse to discourage this harmful behavior?" "Is substance abuse keeping me (us) from family, God, and friends?" Ask yourself, "Am I taking the blame or otherwise enabling my spouse to continue this abuse?"

If you answered "yes" to the above, *get help*. Use the bibliography at the end of this chapter.

40. Find alternatives

Some teens say, "Getting drunk beats boredom." Others say, "I wanted to experiment," and "Everything that's fun is bad, I might as well do this." Encourage your children to fill their spare time with good constructive activity. Good activity promotes physical, mental, and spiritual goodness; on the other hand, bad activity impairs physical, mental, and spiritual well-being. Good constructive activity helps them gain self-confidence and gives them an alternative to drugs and alcohol. Allow your children some independence to entertain themselves, and not have you set up every activity for them. Children who create worthy things to do on their own set a pathway to find good creative drug-free activities in the future. How can you encourage your children to engage in good activities?

...through play?

_____

_____

...through work?

_____

_____

...through school?

_____

_____

...through sports?

_____

_____

...through church?

_____

_____

...through clubs?

_____

_____

...through volunteer projects?

_____

_____

Refrain from letting them choose all the above at once. Children with too many activities become unnecessarily stressed. Stress also becomes an excuse to drink and to get involved in drugs as they grow older.

The "bored" child needs a parent's help. Opposite of what some might think, a simple, God fearing, prayerful, quiet, loving, home atmosphere, where everyone is friendly, not racing to be somewhere and has time to listen, may relieve his boredom.

Children who have a few good friends and activities, have a loving family, and know the Lord should never be bored—or intoxicated.

Addiction

Gradually teach your children to stay away from substance use and abuse long before addiction has a chance to take hold in your family. If someone becomes addicted, though, use outside sources of help.

41. Use caution

Teach your children to be true to themselves. Make them wise about drug dealers, help them have respect for the law and show them how to be cautious about drug and alcohol parties. Drug related gangs could very well come to, or be in your area. Help your children take sides with the good guys.

A drug user's money supports crime in almost every city in the country. In 1 Peter 5:8, it speaks of "a roaring lion, seeking some one to devour." What could you tell your children about why it is wrong to let their money fall into hands of criminals?

_____

_____

_____

_____

Work together with other families and civil authorities to help stop drug distribution and crime. Check with your local school or police department and find out if "neighborhood safety" programs exist, that you can join. Encourage children to tell you about sinister and destructive things. Explain that they should not tell you just to get other people into trouble, but they should do it to prevent someone from harming themselves and others. Listen to your children when they want to talk. Empathize with them as in Exercise 4. Then, as they grow older they will be eager to share their disillusionment about things such as activities of drug pushers.

Describe how you would ask your children to report to the police anyone attempting to sell and use drugs illegally.

_____

_____

_____

_____

If all families reported the illegal drug and alcohol activity they see, how much of a decrease do you think there would be in the availability of drugs in your area and in the exploitation of innocent youth? How would you discuss this with your children?

_____

_____

_____

_____

Tell your children it is a grave sin to drive while under the influence of drugs and alcohol. One might lose a driver's license, go to jail, have an accident, inadvertently kill someone, lose one's life, and worse—lose one's soul. Show your children that adults in their family obey driving laws—and other laws for that matter. When adults obey restrictions, children gain respect for the legal process, and that includes respect for drunk-driving laws. Can you relate an instance in your life when someone either impressed or disillusioned you with their driving ability?

_____

_____

_____

_____

If so, whether or not it involved substance abuse, could this driving instance be a relevant descriptive lesson for teaching your children to drive safely?_____

Parents often wonder how they can get teens to have enough confidence to call them if they become involved in a drug or alcohol party. A reassuring talk with them beforehand is good, although prevention, i.e., raising children to have no need for these parties, is best.

Explain to your children that if they are invited to a party in someone's home or on public or private property, you want to know about it. Tell your children to leave immediately if parents or sponsors are not at the event or if alcohol or drugs are being used. Tell them it's all right to use you as an excuse. Tell your children you want telephone numbers and their exact whereabouts so that you can ensure their safety.

In spite of your warnings, children often wind up at parties where drugs and liquor are the main attraction. Your children need to know of the patience and loving concern you would have if they found themselves in trouble at a party such as this. They also need to know that a telephone call is all it would take for you to arrive in an instant. On the contrary, you cannot interpret patience, loving concern, and rapid help as a means of condoning their actions. It is the means to get them home safely and out of a dire situation. Have you been in any circumstances as a teenager when you wanted your parents to help you, but you were afraid they might get mad?_____ What words and actions could you use to convey to your children you would do the following?

You would be patient and help them in the tough times.

_____

_____

_____

_____

You would expect them to call, and you would be there immediately—no questions asked.

_____

_____

_____

You would talk about their responsibility to God, family, and community after hangovers and tempers had subsided; although, thanking them for removing themselves from a dreadful moment would be the main topic.

_____

_____

_____

Helping them in tough times does not mean that you would protect them from consequences of breaking the law. How could you tell your children, now, that if the law catches them for using drugs and alcohol, you would not over-protect them from school authorities or the police?

_____

_____

_____

One important note for parents is that teens are eager to prove their adulthood, and drinking, unfortunately, is one way they try to prove their maturity. Explain to your children that abusive drinking does not give them a right of passage to adulthood; it grants them a passage to failure. Substance abuse is not an essential part of the high school or college experience. You might say, "Abusive drinking may be a school tradition, but we do not expect you to follow the crowd. We expect you to lead! That is how you prove your adulthood. That is why we send you to school (to be a leader)!" How would you tell your children to *lead* others to do good? (The Cardinal Virtues that our Lord asks of us are prudence [right reason], justice [obedience], fortitude [courage], and temperance [moderation and limits according to law]).

_____

_____

_____

Set curfews depending on age of children; explain that you expect them home at __:___ on weekends and at __:____ on weekdays and that this is subject to change at your command. Your children's safety is contingent on their being true to you, God, and themselves.

42. Find help

Life isn't always the proverbial "bowl of cherries." Sometimes we get addicted. Sometimes it's children, acquaintances, or us. For whatever the circumstance, we need to recognize it so that we can find help.

The capital sins are pride, avarice, envy, wrath, lust, gluttony, and sloth or acedia. These may be connected with addiction in the following ways:

* **Pride** (conceit): Some addicts think only of themselves and no one else. They manipulate and blame others for their problems. They refuse to have the humility to admit their weaknesses and get the help they need.

* **Avarice** (extreme desire for wealth): Drug addicts often need huge amounts of money to support their habits.

* **Envy** (discontent, resentment): They never have quite enough satisfaction from their addiction.

* **Wrath** (anger): Some become annoyed, bitter, and abnormally sensitive. Their home life is in shambles. They nullify themselves and others.

* **Lust** (obsessive desire): They often crave, think, and talk about the substance that abuses their body. Some lie, steal, and cheat to get what they want.

* **Gluttony** (excessive eating or drinking): They overindulge, for instance, to fill an unmet need. Abusers may lose full control even to the detriment of their health, and they cause more problems for themselves than they had in the beginning.

* **Sloth** (lazy) or **acedia** (spiritual boredom or dissatisfaction): The results of long-term drug use are lack of ambition, friendships, faith, reliability, and self-esteem.

We describe people who fit into most of this list as addicted. Explain to your teens the signs of addiction, and how substance abuse is contrary to moral law.

_____

_____

_____

What would you tell your children about this Bible verse, "Whoever does the will of God is my brother, and sister, and mother" (Mark 3:35)?

_____

_____

_____

Be on guard for your children's physical signs of addictive behavior, also. Preoccupation with the drug and alcohol culture, rolling papers, and having small medicine bottles, eyedroppers, pipes, and lighters could signify drug usage. How would you discuss that under no circumstances are they to drink alcohol before the legal age of 21, and they are never to take illegal drugs?

_____

_____

_____

Different stages of drug use range from curiosity, to abuse, to dependence or addiction. Parents must not overreact to the first stages of experimentation and occasional use. Harsh punishment at this stage could push them further into the abusive stages. Consequently, react with loving concern and frank discussion at the first signs of alcohol and drug use. The stages of abuse and dependence, though, require a more advanced plan of action that includes either some or all of the following: discussion, discipline, and outside advice and assistance.

Stage one: Curiosity

For the first time and infrequent user, attempt good discussions.

1) Discussion: Use loving firmness to state the facts and dangers of consumption (from this chapter), and give your expectations; but better yet, ask if they recognize the facts and dangers of alcohol and drug use, and if they identify themselves with higher expectations. Use your empathizing and problem solving skills from Exercise 4. (Sirach 32:1 said to "take good care of them....")

_____

_____

_____

Stage two: Abuse

For an <u>abuser</u> of alcohol and drugs, use discussion and discipline.

1) Discussion (from yourself as above or with a family doctor):

_____

_____

_____

2) Discipline (for example, punishment that fits the offense such as taking the car keys):

_____

_____

_____

Stage three: Addiction

For someone <u>dependent</u> (refer to capital sins, above) on alcohol and drugs, use discussion and discipline (as above), then implement a plan. This requires friends, family, prayer, sacraments, Mass, saints, angels, faith, hope, love, and a coming back to God. Find outside intervention in your Church, the bibliography at the end of this chapter, or the community service section in your telephone directory.

Share with teens the similarity you see between rescuing a drowning victim and taking an alcoholic or drug addict for treatment to a rehabilitation center.

_____

_____

_____

Note: Children who understand spiritual and physical facts, who know parental expectations, and who calculate the consequences of substance abuse more easily fall into <u>positive</u> peer pressure activities:

—where drinking means soda,

—where life-of-the-party means alive-at-the-party, and

—where mingling with the crowd means doing what you think is right and being proud of it!

Endnotes:

1. *Catechism of the Catholic Church* (Washington, D.C.: United States Catholic Conference, 1997) Publication no. 5-110, #2290-#2291, p. 552.

2. "Gambling Impact and Behavior Study," report prepared for the National Gambling Impact Study Commission by National Opinion Research Center of the University of Chicago (April 1, 1999) in collaboration with Gemini Research, Lewin Group, and Christiansen/Cummings Associates, p. viii.

3. "Inhalant Facts for Parents" pamphlet (Lincoln, NE 68508: Alcohol and Drug information Clearinghouse, Nebraska Council to Prevent Alcohol and Drug Abuse, [650 J Street, Suite 215], 1995).

4. *Growing Up Drug Free: A Parents Guide to Prevention*, (Washington D.C., 20202-6123: U.S. Department of Education, Office of Elementary and Secondary Education, Safe and Drug-Free Schools Program, 1998), sources: National Institute on Drug Abuse; Partnership for a Drug-Free America; *Monitoring the Future* Study, 1997; or Drug Enforcement Administration, p. 39.

5. *Get it Straight* (U.S. Department of Justice, Drug Enforcement Administration, 1997), p. 19.

6. *Ibid*, p. 27.

7. *Growing Up Drug Free*, op. cit., sources: National Institute on Drug Abuse; Partnership for a Drug-Free America; *Monitoring the Future* Study, 1997; or Drug Enforcement Administration, p. 34.

8. *Get it Straight*, op. cit., p. 21, 23.

9. *Growing Up Drug Free*, op. cit., p. 15.

10. "Forum," interview with Edward Zigler, Ph. D., Sterling Professor of Psychology and Director of the Bush Center for Child Development and Social Policy at Yale University, *Harvard Mental Health Letter*, Volume 8, Number 4 (October 1991): p. 8.

11. Lauro F. Cavazos, *What Works: Schools Without Drugs* (Pueblo, Co 81009: U.S. Department of Education, 1989), p. 28.

12. *Growing Up Drug Free*, op. cit., sources: National Institute on Drug Abuse; Partnership for a Drug-Free America; *Monitoring the Future* Study, 1997; Drug Enforcement Administration, p. 34.

13. M. David Meagher, *Beginning of a Miracle* (Pompano Beach, Florida 33069: Health Communications, Inc., 1721 Blount Road, 1987), p. 12.

Bibliography:

Al-Anon/Alateen Family Group Headquarters Inc. New York, NY 10018-0862: P.O. Box 862, Midtown Station, Telephone: 1-800-344-2666.

Cavazos, Lauro F., secretary. *What Works: Schools Without Drugs.* Pueblo, CO 81009: The U.S. Department of Education, Telephone: 1-800-624-0100 or call 732-3627 in Washington, D.C., 1989.

Domestic Violence Hotline. Telephone: 1-800-799-7233.

Get it Straight, facts about drug prevention. U.S. Department of Justice, Drug Enforcement Administration, 1997.

Growing Up Drug Free: A Parents Guide to Prevention. Washington D.C., 20202-6123: U.S. Department of Education, Office of Elementary and Secondary Education, Safe and Drug-Free Schools Program, 400 Maryland Avenue, SW, Telephone: 202-260-3954, Web site: www.ed.gov/offices/OESE/SDFS, 1998.

Keeping Youth Drug-Free. U.S. Department of Health and Human Services Substance Abuse and Mental Health Services Admini., Publication No. (SMA) 97-3194, Reprinted 1997.

Family and Home Network, information on parent issues for those who chose to forego or cut back on paid employment to care for their family. Telephone: 1-703-866-4164, Web site: www.familyandhome.org.

National Council on Alcoholism/Drug Dependence, Inc. New York, NY 10010: 12 West 21st Street, 7th Floor, Telephone: 212-206-6770 or 800-NCA-Call, Web site: www.ncadd.org.

The only way you can be positive that your children understand Christian sexual morals is to teach these virtues yourself.

Chapter V

Discuss Sexuality

The Catechism of the Catholic Church explains, 'All the baptized are called to chastity. The Christian has "put on Christ," [Gal 3: 27] the model for all chastity. All Christ's faithful are called to lead a chaste life in keeping with their particular states of life. At the moment of his Baptism, the Christian is pledged to lead his affective life in chastity.'[1]

You would not take classes from a mechanic if you wanted to be a gourmet cook. You would go to a talented friend or a professional. You would find an expert who tempts you with the best food. Too often and without our knowledge, though, our children learn about sexuality from the worst possible sources such as explicit television, magazines, and videos, and those who believe artificial birth control and abortion are the answers to sexual problems. Is it any surprise that statistics skyrocket on sexual abuse, homosexual relationships, sexually transmitted diseases, fornication, and abortion? Is it any surprise that some children (adults, too) lost their taste for innocence?

The only way you can be positive that your children understand Christian sexual morals is to be the expert and teach these virtues yourself. You might expect religious education teachers to teach your children, but they have limits on their time, and they have numerous other topics to cover. To make sure your children's sexuality education is complete, they must hear the truth from you; in fact, the Church expects it. Pray to the Holy Spirit for guidance. In addition, prime your family with pro-life literature on the coffee table and volunteer to pro-life organizations, then you won't be able to stop talking about it.

This chapter is not for children in the natural latency period, approximately ages five to puberty. Beware that one could destroy a child's innocence if sexual pleasure and intercourse are taught during this time. Therefore, (1) *Delicately* discuss with this age group only the answers to questions *they* have about sexuality. Answer their questions in a serious manner, so that they will be open to you in their teen years. You do not, though, have to give detailed answers. Speak simply and according to age level. (2) Discuss how they should avoid certain strangers, and refuse transportation with them. (3) Explain that they are God's gift of life and you love them a lot. Read this chapter yourself, especially Exercises 56 and 57 on "Building a Spiritually Wholesome Sexuality" and implement it into your home life.

On teaching sexual moral convictions to teens, the Church asks us to be truthful, cautious, careful, and in loving honor of the dignity of the person. Never use sensual, suggestive, unworthy, and adulterous ideas. Skim over the chapter. Then, when the time seems appropriate for each young adult, you will be prepared to give adequate moral information to the individual. Instruct in privacy preferably with the parent of the same sex. Be especially mindful to use your own words, and not the script for this chapter. Above all, keep in mind the teachings of the Church. It is not recommended that you teach this chapter all at once. Integrate it with further chapters and with other topics of general Catholic education. You do not want to over-emphasize sexuality education.

This chapter reviews Christian sexuality, chastity, marriage, and more. Determine a time in the young adult years that you think it is proper to teach it. This chapter also reviews natural family planning (NFP). The Catholic Church approves of this form of child spacing. It should merely be explained in terms of *defining* that it is a natural child spacing method for married couples, and it can (not must) be practiced *if* these couples have serious and just reasons to use it. These reasons must not offend the dignity of marriage or the human person. NFP should be used properly, and not outside of marriage or against God's laws. Conversely, the culture wrongly tells us to have intercourse before marriage (with the help of contraceptives) and postpone having children for five years after marriage. This is wrong! You must explain that NFP is not a contraceptive. Again, NFP is not to be used before marriage, and it is to be used only for just and serious reasons after the wedding. You may also want to briefly discuss problems of artificial birth control, abortion, sexually transmitted diseases, and sexual abuse, but without filling their minds with impure acts and words. Instead, instruct mostly on the positive aspects of this chapter by filling their hearts with virtue and good example.

When we follow God's gentle teachings on sexuality, we will not be trapped in the secular dungeons of despair. "For it is by God's will that by doing right you should put to silence the ignorance of foolish men" (1 Peter 2:15).

True Love

The Church asks us to be generous with our time and talents when we choose our vocations in life. Some of the most important vocations are the Sacraments of Marriage and Holy Orders, and the religious vocations. In marriage, we give the total gift of self to our spouse in a life-long covenant of love. Marriage, too, is for family. In Holy Orders or a religious vocation, we give our lifelong covenant of love to the Church and to God.

43. Gift of Self

The *Catechism of the Catholic Church* teaches:

> Charity is the form of all the virtues. Under its influence, chastity appears as a school of the gift of the person. Self-mastery is ordered to the gift of self. Chastity leads him who practices it to become a witness to his neighbor of God's fidelity and loving kindness.[2]

Charitable self-control, then, is the key to the gift of self. With this love and dignity, chastity (pure thoughts and actions) guides us to show our acquaintances about God's loyalty and goodness. Chastity is one of the fruits of the Holy Spirit (there are twelve: charity, joy, peace, patience, kindness, goodness, generosity, gentleness, faithfulness, modesty, self-control, and chastity.) Chastity is not fornication, masturbation, homosexuality, or pornography. It is not contraception, sterilization, or abortion. It is not free love, adultery, divorce, or polygamy.

How would you explain to your teen that chastity means pure actions and pure thoughts, and a love and respect for God, others, and ourselves?

_____

_____

_____

How would you explain to your teen that chastity is the gift of self to our acquaintances, it requires love and self-control, and it is a witness to them of God's devotion and kindness?

_____

_____

_____

Explain to your teens that if anyone tries to tell them there are responsible "choices" other than chastity, they are gravely wrong. Also, explain to teenagers why you will be their sexuality teacher. If a sex education class, however, is mandatory, tell the teacher (parochial or public) you expect to be invited, you want to see the material first, and you will insist that it is not coed. Coed classes create an atmosphere for unsuitable conversation between opposite sexes, and who is to say it won't continue at a time even less appropriate. The other alternatives: exercise your right to say "no," find another school, or homeschool.

44. Vocation of marriage

Christian readiness for the vocation to marriage is not: How many people will stand up for our wedding? How much money will we need before we have children? How can we keep from having a baby? Rather, the following is the best plan for the Sacrament of Marriage as *The Truth and Meaning of Human Sexuality* by the Pontifical Council for the Family points out:

> Formation for true love is always the best preparation for the vocation to marriage. In the family, children and young people can learn to live human sexuality within the solid context of Christian life. They can gradually discover that a stable Christian marriage cannot be regarded as a matter of convenience or mere sexual attraction. By the fact that it is a vocation, marriage must involve a carefully considered choice, a mutual commitment before God and the constant seeking of his help in prayer.[3]

Teenagers may or may not learn about the vocation of marriage from Christian education classes, but prepare yourself so that you can back up what they learned, and reaffirm Church teaching. In the vocation of marriage, a man and woman promise to "love, honor, and obey for richer or for poorer, in sickness and in health, for better or for worse, until death." Spouses are open to fertility and they treat each other with respect without expecting anything in return. They practice purity in their thoughts and actions, and they bring each other to God. Marriage is God's calling to a new realm of sanctity. It is not a mere contract that can be broken; it is a true Christian covenant that cannot be dissolved.

Read together how couples are to prepare for marriage as stated above in *The Truth and Meaning of Human Sexuality*. Purchase a copy listed in the bibliography. Also, find readings about indissolubility of marriage in Matthew 5:31-32 and 19:3-6, and Mark 10:2-12.

How will you tell your young adults about love, marriage, and the joy of having children in Christian life?

_____

_____

_____

_____

45. Vocation of priesthood and religious life

The Church needs vocations to the priesthood and religious life to guide and teach, just as it needs married couples, children, and families to carry on the faith from generation to generation. In a special way, the priesthood and religious life, recognized by the Church, is permanent, and is a call from Christ to perfection. Religious priests, nuns, and brothers profess vows of poverty, chastity, and obedience. Diocesan priests take vows of chastity and obedience. Thereafter, in a supreme way they witness to the kingdom to come.

How can you nurture your son or daughter's calling to the priesthood or religious life? This is what some parents did:

* They said the rosary before bedtime and studied the Bible and Catechism.

* They attended Mass extra times during the week and had special Masses said for vocations.

* They prayed for the gift of vocations, if it is God's will.

* They became friends with priests and spoke of their commitment to renew on the altar the sacrifice of Jesus. They know that to follow Christ means sacrifice. An ordained priest consecrates and offers the body and blood of Christ at the Mass. Priests have the power to forgive sins. Priests and bishops trace their authority back to the apostles.

* They became friends of brothers and spoke of their commitment. (These men live in a religious community, but they do not receive the Sacrament of Holy Orders. Some institutes, however, apply the name of brother to students not yet ordained to the priesthood.)

* They became friends with nuns and spoke of their commitment. (These women live in a community or monastery.)

* They involved children in the Mass as choir members, altar boys, and lectors; they honored the sacraments.

* They toured shrines, churches, and seminaries, and went on pilgrimages.

* They taught them their faith at home and sent them to parochial schools.

* They subscribed to Catholic publications.

* They took part in pro-life activities and lived by it, too. On the contrary, it has been said, the practice of artificial birth control and the lack of generosity contribute to the dearth of religious vocations. [4]

* They have families that show concern for people in all levels of society.

* They have fathers who take the job as head of the household seriously. A good provider, in turn, produces male children who are good providers, whether it be as a father (in marriage) for his own children, or as a "Father" (priest) for all God's children.

* They have mothers who take the job of nurturing children seriously. A mother who bonds well with her children produces children who respect motherhood in marriage, and respect the Church as mother.

How would you tell your son or daughter about love and commitment in the priesthood or religious life?

_____

_____

_____

_____

How would you explain to them that if they chose this vocation, you would support their choice?

_____

_____

_____

_____

Circle the ways, above, you could encourage your children to consider the religious life.

For information on discerning marriage, priesthood, and religious life, find "Vocations Congress" and "Catholic Singlesin the bibliography at end of this chapter.

Chastity

God explained his beautiful plan when he said, "'Be fruitful and multiply and fill the earth....'" (Genesis 1:28). He did not mean increase teen sexual relations, multiply diseases, and fill the earth with every type of deviant behavior! He meant we should beget children in a chaste manner within the marriage covenant.

Here is what an experienced volunteer for a crisis pregnancy center noted: "I learned that unmarried sexually active girls seeking pregnancy tests were for the most part open, willing to talk, and eager to listen. Yet, they believed their sexual lifestyle was the right thing to do and even expected of them." This immoral behavior is wrong.

Our young people hunger for the truth and we must give it to them. Again, with virtue and good example, teach your children about sexuality.

46. Meaning of freedom

Teach your teenagers about sexuality and marriage when you believe they are ready to learn—and especially if they say they "know everything." A father/son or mother/daughter talk is needed. Each child learns at a slightly different age. They do not need to know about sexual pleasure. Decide which of the following you need to teach your teens, and when:

_____ How God fills the land with precious, blessed children through the incredible value of a father and mother. Isaiah 49:15 on the worth of a child says, "...Even these may forget, yet I will not forget you." (Read all of Isaiah 49 together.)

_____ The differences between love, lust, and sex (or intercourse): Love is perseverant, compassionate, generous, act of the will and not just a feeling; lust is self-gratification; and sexual intercourse is a physical act of self-giving appropriate only within the Sacrament of Matrimony.

_____ The meaning of chastity and the importance of marriage before sexual relationship. (The Bible refers to chastity and marriage in I Corinthians 7:8-11; Exodus 20:14,17.) Chastity and sexual intercourse inside marriage is like a quiet brook; sex outside marriage is like having the brook flood your house, which is disastrous.

_____ The importance of Christian marriage within the Church; that is, the permanent union and fidelity between husband and wife, and the responsibility to care for and educate children within that union. Colossians 3:18-21 describes the Christian family.

_____ Why sexual jokes and ludicrous sexual remarks are a form of harassment to the opposite sex and are never in good taste.

Unfortunately, some teens learn most of their sexuality education from outsiders and that is the end of their formal education. You can make a difference.

You may choose to do something special, such as lunch, tennis, or fishing on the days you talk with your teenager. Another teaching moment may be when the rest of the family has settled down for the night, and you have some time alone with a particular teen. Your child may be embarrassed and act as if they don't want to talk about sexuality. Be calm and state that this is an important subject. Explain that you want him or her to hear it from you because many secular sources may try to state something different.

How would you explain to your teenager that following God's will in the virtue of chastity takes much spiritual and parental guidance, and prayer?

_____

_____

_____

_____

The world bombards us with the idea of casual sex, but seldom do we hear about the virtue of chastity. When we practice chastity, we control our desire for sexual pleasure and conform it to faith and right reason. When married couples practice chastity, they temper their desire to their state of life. Single people, however, refrain from sexual relationships until they are married. For those who do not marry, they sacrifice their desire completely.

Teach teens how chastity is a virtue, pleasing to God, that everyone must cultivate to develop love for someone. We gain this virtue by practicing the other fruits of the Holy Spirit, too, especially modesty, charity, and self-control, mentioned in Exercises 43 and 60. Again, we must act in accordance to faith and right reason. When we aren't chaste, we don't love God, friends, or ourselves. Chastity is not only abstinence from sexual relations in the religious life, and outside of marriage, it is purity of body, mind, and soul, at all times. "You have heard that it was said, 'You shall not commit adultery.' But I say to you that every one who looks at a woman lustfully has already committed adultery with her in his heart" (Matthew 5:27-28). In your own words, talk about this definition of chastity.

_____

_____

_____

_____

After reviewing a Justice Department National Survey, "Female Victims of Violent Crime," Michael McManus stated that couples who lived together before marriage had "a 50 percent higher divorce rate than for non-cohabitants." In addition, he said, "…of 100 trial marriages, only 15 get lasting marriages"[5] How would you explain this to your teens?

_____

_____

_____

_____

47. Advantages of chastity

The advantages of chastity are many. Sometimes young people are unsure when they must practice chastity. They may feel that sexual relations are okay when they have dated for three months, or perhaps when they are engaged. They do not always understand what is expected of them; therefore, here is a breakdown of the moral necessity of chastity in whatever state of courtship they enter.

Impurity and sexual relations outside marriage in <u>**casual dating relationships**</u> hurt women, men, and children, but chastity brings:

* Joy of harmony with God's laws of morality and self-control. "…The body is not meant for immorality…" (1 Corinthians 6:13).

* Freedom to love another, not for sex but for who you are. If you can say no to sex outside marriage, you can say yes to love.

* Liberty from sexually transmitted diseases—refer ahead to Exercise 53.

* Independence from using immoral and harmful, abortive, or defective contraceptive pills, shots, and devices. Refer to Exercise 60.

* Avoidance of being a single parent and the poverty that often goes with it.

* Self-respect and freedom from guilt and emotional complications.

* Release from sexual exploitation.

* Ability to know and have fun with many different friends of the opposite sex.

* Liberation from the pain of broken sexual relationships and liberation, therefore, from reasons to become depressed and to begin drinking and using drugs.

* Leisure to let love take its course and find a spouse who respects you and your future family.

* Knowledge that you are loved unconditionally and not for only the way you perform sexually.

* Fun of dreaming about a future marriage with a once-in-a-lifetime committed spouse.

At what age do you want your teens to know about the problems of promiscuity versus the advantages of chastity while dating?_____

Circle any of the above ideas you want to share with your teenagers.

Chastity brings to **engaged couples** all the above plus:

* The ability to save their virginity for another potential marriage partner in case the engagement breaks.

* The ability to prove to each other that if they can obey the laws of chastity outside marriage, then they will also obey the laws of chastity inside marriage.

* Romance, such as, walking on the beach and whispering "I-love-you's" to each other. Romance solidifies and beautifies mutual respect for each other.

* Ability to spend more time getting to know each other by planning family activities, communicating, holding hands, being alone in public places, expressing feelings, being best friends, and occasionally kissing.

* A chance to prove they recognize each other because of their physical, spiritual, and intellectual abilities and not because of their sexual performance.

* A realization that sex is a consummation of the marital commitment.

Circle the above ideas you would share with teenagers.

Chastity before marriage and sexual relations with only one's spouse brings to **married couples**:

* Peace of mind that one's spouse can remain faithful during periods of being separated when a child is born, when there is sickness, when there are just reasons for limiting the size of the family, and so forth. "Blessed is every one who fears the Lord.... Your wife will be like a fruitful vine...your children will be like olive shoots..." (Psalm 128:1-3).

* Children who feel secure because their parents are faithful to each other.

* A solid relationship, less prone to divorce.

Circle ideas, above, you want to share with young adults when the time seems right. If they have "locker room friends" or pals that begin dating early, you may have to discuss it then. Have them list reasons for chastity they believe are important, such as desire not to commit mortal sin. Make clear that Jesus is the *main* reason we practice chastity. Ask them to pledge to be modest inside and outside of marriage. Have them write the promise on a special letter or note card and keep it in an envelope.

48. Prevent fornication

Engaging in sexual relationships outside marriage is destructive, hurtful, and degrading. Parents must be on guard to avoid this seduction from happening with their children. One preventive measure comes through adequate supervision, another through communication. Fornication often results when children are unsupervised at home, and also when they are oblivious as to what is expected of them.

Most families want one parent to stay at home with their children, and they find it difficult because of financial problems. There is usually no better substitute than having a mom or dad at home, even if both need to work split shifts or if one takes an at-home job. Bonding and obeying go together. If you bond with your children, the chances are excellent that they will obey your rules and your morals. If full-time parenthood is not possible, then you could fill your children's lonely, idle hours with a baby-sitter, after school programs, neighborhood supervision, after school jobs, hobbies, and more. If your children (this includes adolescents and teens) need attention and support, how can you overcome the situation?

_____

_____

_____

_____

You can find help for the stay-at-home-mother who needs financial assistance. Books, services, and a newsletter are available in the bibliography at the end of this chapter.

You might have difficulty with unmarried teenagers who bought into the idea of the sexual revolution. Explain how God wants us to be responsible and to love and have children inside the covenant of marriage. "Therefore a man leaves his father and his mother and cleaves to his wife, and they become one flesh" (Genesis 2:24).

Your children may say they do not believe that sex is only for marriage. They might say, "It's my life. I'll do what I want." In this case, go back to Exercise 25, and talk about the SCARE acronym. Review the secrecy, control, addiction, ridicule, and excuses they may be using to get what they want. Then discuss, again, Exercises 43 and 44 on chastity.

You could respond with, "Where might this lead? What could it do to you and your friend? What does this do to the soul? Never mind about teen pregnancy. I don't care if condoms work; you are using it for sexual gratification. What are the consequences of your actions when you refuse to follow what God says? What kind of role model do you want to be for your future family?" How would you show your child the true dignity of his humanity (see Exercises 1 and 2 if needed)?

_____

_____

_____

_____

Let your young adult read Mark 5:1-20 and see how "no one had the strength to subdue him...." except Jesus; or read about Revelation 13 and "the beast...[who] deceives those who dwell on earth..."; or examine Mark 10:19, the commandments.

How would you explain the difference between God-like and beast-like behavior of sexuality to your child? (Follow Exercises 22 and 23.)

_____

_____

_____

_____

The purpose of being male or female is to permanently give ourselves to another either in marriage to a spouse, or in the priesthood or religious life to God. In this way, we become parents either physically or spiritually. How would you tell your children that God has a plan for their life, and you wouldn't want them to mess it up by abusing their sexuality (and someone else's, too) through fornication?

_____

_____

_____

_____

Let your children know in spite of all their chastity education, and in spite of all their understanding of the reasons for saying "no," sometimes kids blunder and lose their virginity. Reiterate your hope that this never happens, but that you will be with them in their brokenness. Tell them that you hope they learn something by their mistakes, go to confession to clear their conscience, tell God they are sorry, and make amends. Explain what a superb future they have if they repent and follow Jesus.

49. Protect oneself from abuse

Scholastic Choices Magazine reported, "In a study by University of California, Los Angeles researchers, more than half of the teen boys and almost half of the teen girls surveyed thought it was OK for a boy to force sex on a girl if she excites him sexually."[6] You can help your children be aware of misconceptions by preparing yourself with good responses. Teach children to defend themselves from rape, date rape, incest, child abuse, lewdness, and harassment in the following ways:

* Dress modestly and avoid dark, lonely, questionable, and strange places when either indoors or out.

* Refuse to give information to strangers on the telephone, never give them entry into your home or car, and stand a distance away from them.

* Confide in parents and call home when something doesn't seem right. Your parents won't be mad. They will be happy to help you in times of need. Your parents will be patient and reassuring.

* Know the Christian truth that sexual relationship is immoral outside of marriage. Even government laws are somewhat similar—one law states it is illegal for a man 19 and older to have intercourse with a girl 16 and younger. This is both spiritual and civil requirement.

* Be with people you trust. Be cautious of at least some acquaintances, especially if they are inebriated. Rapists aren't always strangers. Often they make it a point to be extra friendly. A "Rape Facts and Prevention" report reveals, "As many as 4/5 of the victims will know their attacker."[7] You can reduce chances of rape if you avoid being alone with your date, if you date in groups, if you know the background of your dates, and if you refrain from alcohol and drugs.

* Refuse transportation with strangers even if they either appear friendly or accost you with a gun. Yell, bite, and kick until you gain help. Victims are safer outside of cars even if threatened. Abductors may trick you to go near their car by saying their dog got lost, they need the groceries carried out, or their mom told him to pick them up. Stand your distance, and get a parent's permission before you go with even those who appear refined.

* Be assertive and demand respect even if someone spent much money on you, and date those individuals who themselves have self-respect. A date that is jealous,

controlling, blaming, cruel, verbally abusive, angry, threatening, violent, and forceful even part of the time is no prize. Put God in control, not your partner.

* Avoid punchbowls and soft drinks left unattended. Someone might spike these with alcohol or drugs. A Columbia University survey found, "90% of all reported campus rapes occur when alcohol is being used by either the assailant, the victim, or both."[8] Stay away from liquor and drugs. One drug is called a "Date Rape Drug," Rohypnol, sometimes called Roofies, Roche, Rope, Ruffies, R-2, Roaches, Rib, and Mexican Valium. It can unknowingly be added to liquor and other drugs.

* Stay away from people who preoccupy themselves with sexual jokes, pictures, films, and recordings. (Matthew 6:22 says, their whole being becomes dark.)

* Know that avoidance is not enough; abusers often continue to abuse until an outsider intervenes.

Circle the precautions you want to discuss with your teens, now. Next, put an X on the ones you want to discuss and repeat in the future.

50. Discuss abuse and SCARE

Mary Koss, professor at the University of Arizona Medical School's Psychiatry Department, reported: "One woman in four over age 14 has been the victim of rape or attempted rape…"[9] Women are at risk. Here are additional ideas about teaching your children to protect themselves.

No one (neither relative, stranger, boyfriend, nor girlfriend) has the right to have charge of (or play with) another person's body, especially under their clothing and in the bathing suit areas. At what age do you think it would be appropriate to tell your children about avoiding this aspect of sexual abuse?_____ How would you tell them to say "no" and move away even if the person gets mad at them?

_____

_____

_____

Boys as well as girls are the victims of abuse, and both need knowledge of how to avoid being sexually controlled. Describe sexual abuse (casual sex, rape, date rape, incest, child abuse, and sexual harassment) without making your child unduly afraid. Use newspaper stories (one or two might be enough) and avoid incidents of close acquaintances. Your child may get the messages, "It's a terrible world," and "Everyone is doing it, so why am I different?" Go easy on this subject, but do talk about it. Write down a recent abuse story or two that you want to discuss with your teenager.

_____

_____

_____

_____

_____

From the above, show your child how some or all of the perpetrator's SCARE tactics (as described in Exercise 21) listed below could help the victim recognize this situation. Use some imagination, since you may not know all of the story's facts.

Secrecy_____

Control_____

Addiction_____

Ridicule_____

Excuses/Enemies_____

Ask your teen how the people above might have prevented being abused by using one or two of the following responses.

Take time to sort through the facts

_____

Respond with patience, persistence, and tact

_____

Find alternatives

_____

Ask questions

_____

Use caution

_____

You must make it clear to your children that victims of abuse are not at fault. Your children then should not feel unnecessarily guilty if something happens.

Rape and abuse are the faults of the abuser, not the abused. They should notify the proper authorities at once, so that prosecution and rehabilitation of the abuser begins immediately.

Your telephone book lists additional help in the community service section under "Abuse."

51. Discuss pornography

Pornography devastates children. Preoccupation with it leads us to disrespect our own selves and others, too. It is a sin against God, and it turns other people into objects and robs them of their dignity. In extreme cases, it is the root cause in numerous crimes of rape, incest, murder, and other heinous crimes. How can you warn your teens about obscenity? Caring and concerned statements such as, "I want" and "I expect" as suggested in Exercise 4 can help.

_____

_____

Kids are curious about pornography. Try not to react in extreme ways: Reading directly from the Bible or scolding them may not be good discipline for a child who has just discovered nude pictures. Explain to your children that it is their duty to protect their purity by controlling what they watch, read, think about, and listen to. It is also their responsibility not to exploit others by turning them into sex objects that we view to gratify our curiosity or lust.

_____

_____

_____

_____

What positive steps can you take against pornography in your area?

_____

_____

52. Discuss masturbation

Masturbation is a sin because it is outside of the moral order, it is an act of self-gratification, and it is a misuse of our bodies. Rev. Robert J. Fox, author of _Charity, Morality, Sex, and Young People_ said:

> [Masturbation] is a misuse of sex, a turning in on one's self....A person who has this problem is not abnormal or strange. He must,

however, learn to control his passions and his sexual urges. He needs strong will power and he needs the help of God....Sex is sacred and not just for fun.[10]

Just as ripping the leaves off an apple tree destroys the dignity of the tree, masturbation destroys the dignity of those who use it. Controlling the urge to masturbate requires turning away from any sexually explicit performances, films, and magazines that excite one sexually, and it requires asking God to help us understand pure actions, thoughts, and desires. Masturbation is not to be confused with nocturnal emission.

If you have a need to teach this to a child, how would you tell them that masturbation is selfish and wrong?

_____

_____

_____

53. Stop sexually transmitted diseases

These diseases are often incurable, permanently damaging, and deadly. They are now an epidemic in this country precisely because many people live unchaste lives. Those infected with STDs transmit it to their partners. The symptoms can vary from no visible indications (STDs are contagious and unhealthy even if one has no visible symptoms) to many signs, such as itching, sores, warts, rashes, burning urination, discharge, fever, sore throat, and hair loss. Millions developed the fast-spreading AIDS virus. Millions more contacted other STDs. G.D. Searle & Company said, "All partners must be treated simultaneously to avoid reinfection."[11] For some, however, there is no cure. Symptoms, complications, and treatments of several STDs (there are many others) follow:

* **Chlamydia**: According to the Parke-Davis Company, chlamydia is "the number one sexually transmitted disease in the United States,..." They pointed out, "Chlamydia is very serious, but unlike other sexually transmitted diseases, you may not know you have it....This bacteria may cause a variety of disorders, including pelvic inflammatory disease (PID) in women, urethritis in men, and pneumonia in newborn infants of infected mothers." Further complications are "chronic pelvic pain, ectopic (tubal) pregnancy, and infertility. In men, chlamydia can damage the epididymis (a part of the testes), leading to sterility." It is treated with antibiotics.[12] At what age do you think you should have a discussion with your teen about STDs?___ Explain how difficult life could be if one contacted an

STD. Proverbs 7:1-27 tells about a "young man without sense" and a "loose woman" and "death."

* __Gonorrhea__: Symptoms in women, as recorded by the Center for Disease Control, are "a painful or burning sensation when urinating, increased vaginal discharge, or vaginal bleeding between periods. Women with no or mild gonorrhea symptoms are still at risk of developing serious complications from the infection." They can more easily get pelvic inflammatory disease that "can cause infertility or can damage the fallopian tubes enough to increase the risk of ectopic pregnancy." A woman "may give the infection to the baby." "Gonorrhea can spread to the blood or joints. This condition can be life threatening" in both men and women. Symptoms occurring in men include: "a burning sensation when urinating, or a white, yellow, or green discharge from the penis. Sometimes men with gonorrhea get painful or swollen testicles." It is treated with "antibiotics."[13] Getting this increasingly drug-resistant sexually transmitted disease demonstrates our weakness to carnal desires. Anyone who has had intercourse outside of marriage needs to be checked by a doctor, must turn their life back to God, and choose chastity. This lifestyle change is called secondary virginity. Express to your children that God will help us through our weakness if we love him, repent, and ask forgiveness. Mark 8:36-38 talks about sin and adultery.

* __Trichomoniasis__: According to G.D. Searle & Co., "Women...[have either] yellow or green frothy discharge with an offensive odor. Burning and itching sensations are common." They said, "some women can be asymptomatic carriers. Men rarely have symptoms." It is treated by "medication."[14] Explain to teenagers why you think exposing oneself to sexually transmitted diseases through unmarried sexual relations is contrary to human dignity.

* __Venereal Warts__: G. D. Searle & Co. said, "Internal warts remain undetected until they cause discomfort, such as mild irritation or itching....In men there are usually few or no symptoms." Complications: Women may develop "pain during intercourse..." complications during pregnancy, and "cervical cancer." It is treated with "topical chemical," surgery, burning, and "alpha-interferon."[15]— Ask young adults if this STD caused by human papilloma virus seems unfair to women. Explain how you feel about it. Would the man feel some effects, too, such as guilt, and in some cases grief over losing a mate to cancer.

* __Herpes__: A Planned Parenthood publication said the patient has "[p]ainful blisters...[and] open sores. Sores usually appear on or near the mouth, sex organs, or rectum. They may be found on a woman's cervix (inside her vagina) where she may not notice them." Complications: "Infection can be passed to newborn, causing it serious illness or death." Treatment is with "acyclovir." "There is no

known cure…"[16]—Explain to your children that you would not want to pass a disease onto your spouse that has no cure.

* <u>Syphilis</u>: Searle and Co. says sores [chancres] are often found in women in the vaginal area and are hard to detect at first. In men the chancre forms externally in the genital area. After a chancre is gone, a person may develop "weakness, slight fever, or a rash on the body…." Complications: Syphilis may cause "blindness, heart disease…insanity, tumors, death, stroke," and "miscarriages, stillbirth, or congenital syphilis…." Treatment of "penicillin" cures but does not reverse damage.[17]—Explain to your child that even though modern medicine can cure some STDs, it cannot cure all of them, and it cannot restore spiritual well-being.

* <u>AIDS</u>: According to the U.S. Centers for Disease Control, it is "a disease caused by a virus that can damage the brain and destroy the body's ability to fight off illness." Complications: "[I]t allows other infections (such as pneumonia, cancer, and other illnesses) to invade the body, and these diseases can kill." Treatment includes "no known cure…and no vaccine that prevents the disease."[18] Various drugs recently show remarkable progress. Note: Those contagious with the AIDS virus remain asymptomatic for the first five or ten years during which time they can unknowingly infect others either sexually or through the transfer of blood products. Most STDs are asymptomatic at one time or another. Help children understand how easy it would be to get infected from a partner if they didn't know their partner had AIDS or another STD. According to international statistics, an estimated 3 million people die each year of AIDS.[19] This is more than the number of people living in Chicago.

If one equates condom usage to preventing STDs, it would be as if we gave children rubber suits for swimming in contaminated lakes. Condoms provide little help compared to abstinence. A moment of passion isn't worth a lifetime of spiritual and physical misery. For prevention, instruct them about purity, and tell them you would take them to a *pro-life* doctor if they needed STD testing.

"Gift of Love" listed in the bibliography at end of this chapter helps homeless AIDS patients, and "One More Soul" helps you find pro-life doctors.

Marriage and Courtship

Teens need you as a role model for marriage. They also need clear directions on dating and marriage. Sending young adults on dates and into marriage without guidance is as dangerous as letting them fly an airplane without prior instruction.

54. Understand marriage relationship

Long before your children begin dating, you naturally teach them how marriage works. In other words, you try to set a good example. Good marriages and happy families abound (an important note to make to children), but so do broken and unhappy ones. We must explore all possible means of preventing divorce and try to keep marriages intact. Broken marriages cause untold grief, depression, rejection, poverty, and abandonment for parents as well as children. On the other hand, good Christian marriages (where husbands are the head and wives are the heart of the family) are a source of unity, love, respect, and peace in the home and consequently in society. The marriage you and your spouse have, or wish you could have had, acts as a mirror to your children. One compliment from your spouse lasts a lifetime—one criticism lasts a lifetime, too, unless it is repented. Each day, you can teach children about good marriage from your actions and words. This is the *first* school of love.

Even if you do not have a perfect union, you can try to build a good one. The definition of a strong family is not one that is free of anxiety, strife, or disagreement; rather, it is one that has energy, fortitude, and faith to overcome problems. Make a choice to love; make an agreement to maintain composure when your spouse loses it. Avoid critical remarks—even the smallest kind. Discussion and forgiveness, not conflict, is key to solving disputes. Because good marriage isn't easy, it doesn't mean it can't survive. A good business isn't made in a day; neither is a good marriage. It involves Christian sacrifice.

Discuss with your children how marriage is wonderful, and yet sometimes you do have conflicts. Tell how you expect them to enter marriage with the idea that you will work it out, get help if necessary, and plan to stay married forever with the blessings of God and his Church.

Instead of looking back at a fight, a criticism, a misunderstanding, a mistake, or a failure, deal with it quickly and then look forward to the next hug, Christmas tree, Sunday (or daily) Mass, little league game, sunset, ice cream cone, and joke. Love is a choice. Parents who live by their faith convictions, receive the sacraments often, kiss each other good-bye in the morning, hold hands, show appreciation, take leisure time together, or plan dates for Friday nights are doing kind acts for each other. Thus, they teach simple, important lessons of marriage to their children. They replicate God's desire and forgiveness. Explain to your children that it takes love and determination to make a marriage strong.

_____

_____

_____

Could it be that setting priorities, making life more simple, and having more time for your family would make a huge difference in your own happiness, as well as in the happiness in your marriage and in your family? "...He who loves his wife, loves himself." Ephesians 5:28. How would you share this Scripture and the above ideas with your children?

_____

_____

_____

Learn to exchange positive communication with your spouse with <u>what</u>, <u>where</u>, <u>how</u>, and <u>when</u> questions and <u>I</u> statements, as in the following:

Instead of saying, "We never get to see my family," say, "When could we go to see my folks?"

Instead of saying, "You never help me," say, "I'm too tired tonight to put the kids to bed."

Instead of saying, "Why is this house always such a mess?" say, "What shall we do about these toys?"

Instead of saying, "We're always late!" say, "How can I help us get to church on time?"

Instead of saying, "Why can't you ever help me?" say, "I need the chores done that are posted on the refrigerator. Could we work together on this, or get a cleaning lady?"

When you state facts and ask questions, it gives you a chance to listen to what your spouse has to say. After you practice positive communication and listening for a few months, your marriage will be greatly improved. Kind words join you and your spouse as respectful partners. Without criticism, both of you are free to iron out problems; with criticism, though, only one person works at a solution—the other is tuned out. Give it time. You cannot reform another person if they are not open to it, but you can impress them with your patience, kindness, and good example.

Another marriage strengthener is natural family planning (NFP) when used for just reasons. In contrast, artificial birth control has a negative spiritual influence on marriage because it stands between love and life. Chemical birth control, too, causes emotional damage to marriage relationships. Read about artificial birth control ahead in Exercise 60 and you will find the reasons. In Exercise 59, though, find help, if needed, with Church approved, marriage strengthening NFP.

From the examples above, relate some times when you have shown your children that marriage is beautiful, family oriented, and God-based. Discuss this with them.

_____

_____

_____

Even if there is brokenness and divorce in the family, talk to your children about what went wrong and how you plan to make the best of the situation. Relate your ideas of a good (not perfect) marriage, and discuss the role that husbands, wives, and children have in the home. Children want to understand marriage relationships, they want to know both parents love them (if possible), and they want to comprehend that they will not be left without a home, and they want to associate with people who have two-parent homes. Relate experiences, good and bad, that you could share with your children. Impress on them the importance of good marriage and tell of how you tried to make it work, perhaps through the help of a priest, counselor, confessor, family member, or special friend.

_____

_____

_____

55. Set dating guidelines

Teens need guidance especially on the subject of dating. Train them to know the facts, to think ahead, and to make good judgments before they become serious about a future spouse.

Single and steady dating is dangerous in junior high school (and it should be discouraged even in high school)—ask any parent of an unmarried, promiscuous teenage son or daughter. Single dating at young ages (especially under 17 or 18 years of age) paves the pathway to a dangerous relationship. Relate to your children how old you want them to be when they begin dating in groups._____...courting as single couples thinking of marriage._____

The purpose of courting is to become acquainted with a potential spouse who is prepared to be either a loving, nurturing mom, or a providing, caring dad. On the other hand, dating and getting serious about marriage with the first person that looks at you is often a mistake. How would you discuss this with your children?

_____

_____

Eventually, most young adults do become serious about someone. Discuss how to avoid near occasions of sin and remain pure in thoughts, words, and actions. Remember the thought-provoking questions, and "I want" and "I expect" statements of Exercise 4. Discuss with them the following proper courting practices:

Having respect for oneself and for one's friend

_____

_____

Entertaining a date in the home with the family

_____

_____

Staying out of empty houses when parents are not at home, and staying out of bedrooms altogether

_____

_____

Choosing moral entertainment and modest clothing

_____

_____

Obeying curfews

_____

_____

Choosing a simple kiss or no kiss at all

_____

_____

Not remaining in a parked car but coming into the house

_____

_____

Dating in groups and never dating steady in high school

_____

_____

Finding a date (gals, wait for the guy to ask) who loves God more than self

_____

_____

Never courting with the idea of changing the other person (it seldom happens); instead, pray and stay away until they change themselves with the help of God

_____

_____

Looking for character and not only for looks

_____

_____

Choosing a spouse who is kind, and patient, and obedient to God; a wife that models Mary or a husband that exemplifies Joseph

_____

_____

Refusing to drink alcohol or use illegal drugs

_____

_____

Focusing not on sinful pleasures of the moment, but on our Lord Jesus Christ, now and forever

_____

_____

Staying distant from those that would lead you *away* from your faith, and instead choosing a spouse who would lead your future family *in* the faith

_____

_____

Attending only chaperoned parties

_____

_____

Staying away from courting the divorced unless they are free to marry through an annulment (Divorce and remarriage constitutes adultery unless an annulment is granted.)

_____

_____

Explain to your children how anyone who disrespects them also has no respect for themselves or God. Your children should understand that they must cautiously stay away from rude people. Encourage your children to talk with you and to enlist help from the Holy Spirit, Blessed Virgin Mary, the saints, and guardian angels!

Build a Spiritually Wholesome Sexuality

Married couples may use some of this section on spirituality *before* they have children—it is that important. Implement this into daily living. Use it whether your children are two or twenty-two. You can give your children the best sex education in the world. You can sit and talk to them until you can't talk anymore. You can expound on every detail until there is nothing left uncovered. The fundamental root, however, of affirming a spiritually wholesome sexuality in your children lies in seeking faith and then living it out.

56. Seek the faith

Planting faith in children and saying "no" to a pagan culture begins before tots are born. It is like planting corn. You prepare a good seedbed, so that corn grows tall and straight. Likewise, in the following ways, you begin a strong spiritual growth, so that family faith flourishes:

* Start each day with the "Morning Offering." It is in the prayer section at the back of this book. Dedicate each day to Jesus through the Immaculate Heart of Mary.

* Avoid distraction and ask Mary to guide you in purity to the Sacred Heart of Jesus in every thought, word, and action of the day. Do this for as long as you live.

* Take faith seriously. It is serious sin to willfully miss a Mass on Sundays and Holy Days. Lent and Advent, too, are good times to practice our faith. When we

miss excellent opportunities to obey Church teachings, it relays the idea to our children that there are exceptions to every rule.

* Listen to God often throughout the day. Make him a part of your daily life. Let your children know that faith doesn't happen only once a week.

* Sign up for a Holy Hour at your Church. If Holy Hours haven't been established, ask your priest if you could start one. You can obtain a booklet *Holy Hour of Reparation* listed in the bibliography. This is one of their Holy Hour prayers: "The more sin and impurity destroy the image of God in man, the more we shall try by purity of life to be a living temple of the Holy Ghost, O Heart of Jesus!"[20] The booklet asks you to spend one hour in prayer and reparation each week before the tabernacle.

* The Church says we must pray and sacrifice for the betterment of all human life. Offer your prayers (especially the rosary) and sufferings to the Lord for the difficult times of others—the poor, sick, addicted, dying, divorced, unborn, pregnant teen mother, AIDS victims, and so forth.

* Make reparations for sins. Go to Penance and Holy Communion often. Refuse to let evil darken the soul. Respect what the Church says against infidelity, contraception, abortion, euthanasia, and other issues that are not pro-life. Show your family that you believe all life is sacred and all people are made in the image and likeness of God, our Almighty Father. Make it clear that you will pray and strive for a spotless soul.

* Refuse to buy into the culture. We have senseless authorities telling us there is no sin connection between the AIDS epidemic and promiscuous sexual transmission of it. We have other so-called experts telling our children there is a new "responsible" definition of morality. We even have reprehensible people telling us that bishops are too strict against pro-abortion politicians. Read what the *Splendor of Truth* has to say about this phenomenon:

> ...there have developed *certain interpretations of Christian morality which are not consistent with "sound teaching"* (2 Timothy 4:3).[21]

Ask the Dear Lord to send the Holy Spirit down on our families and save them from the wars on their homes. Ask him to bless all parents and give them special graces through prayer and good works to teach their children to lead God's army in purity. Ask God to bless, especially, the struggling family, the one that has been fragmented by the culture, and torn to shreds by the experts of irrationalism and the New Age. Ask the Dear Lord to lead them in special ways, back to the spirituality and goodness of his promises.

Whether or not you have children, you can implement any of the above ideas into your home life. Circle the ones you might do now. From items above, what would you discuss with your teenagers about planting faith in their future families if they choose to marry?

_____

_____

_____

57. Live the faith

Now, with a background of prayer, bring other good works into your family household such as love, joy, security, dignity, and balance. Here is how you can help your children grow in faith and purity in spite of the sexual revolution:

* Love your children, especially moms and girls, and dads and boys. Touch them, hug them, talk to them, and resolve conflict. Remind them often of how much you love them, and tell them of the joy they bring to the family. Then, they will not have to find love elsewhere in the wrong places.

* Live according to God's plan and be joyful with family in stressful times. Teach children to follow Jesus and love, help, and respect others in need, even if it requires pain and hard work. This is the meaning of true happiness. Find more on this at "Center for Life Principles"in the bibliography.

* Help your children understand the nature of men and women. Dads are the head of the household; moms are the heart of the household. Society tried to turn that around. It failed miserably. Dads naturally have the instinct to provide for their families. They work at jobs outside the home. They repair the car (or have it repaired) if needed. Their interest lies in the soil, roof, water pipes, and plumbing. They are more concerned about where the food, water, and shelter come from, than how it serves us once we get it. Moms, on the other hand, carry a child for nine months. She becomes bonded to that child even before she delivers it. She knows exactly (well, usually) what the child needs when it cries. She senses when children are in trouble. She has the natural instinct to feel sad when they are sad and glad when they are glad. God made us this way. Of course, there are variances in each family; however, God had a basic design for men and women and it has lasted for centuries. Remind children that attempts to break that design often lead to disaster within the family, as the last century has proven. Children need firm loving moms and authoritative, caring dads.

* Marriage and parenting are seldom recognized as valid vocations by modernists. Prove them wrong. Raising a family is one of the most dignified jobs in the world! Mother Teresa expressed, "How can there be too many children? That is like saying there are too many flowers." Dare to turn secularism around and concentrate, instead, on the family.

* Have faith in your children that they follow the Lord. Explain how they have special purpose on this earth: to know, love, and serve the Lord.

* Find help if there has been sexual abuse in the family. You might explain to children that abusers have not obeyed the "Cardinal Virtues" of prudence, justice, fortitude, and temperance that all Christians are obliged to follow.

* Help children have balance in work, play, school, friendships, and responsibility. Too much of one thing may not be a good idea, especially if they join the wrong crowd.

Circle any of the above that may be essential to your family at this time.

How would you talk to your teens about developing the strengths noted above in their future families?

_____

_____

_____

It takes faith and good works to make a house a home.

Natural Family Planning, Birth Control, Abortion, and More

This section covers the beauty of the gift of life and of natural family planning (NFP), versus the violations and fallacies of artificial birth control, abortion, and euthanasia. Help children know that artificial birth control and abortion will not cure teenage pregnancy—pregnancy isn't a disease, it is a precious child. Show them support and courage to avoid the sexual revolution that brought us broken homes, disease, death, and more.

58. Affirm the gift of life

A child is a human being from the moment of conception (moment of fertilization). There is no other way about it. Secular humanists would prefer to call a baby a "blob of tissue" or a "product of conception." Some scientists call fertilization of a baby an experiment—anything to make it seem less human. Others would not call a baby a human being until it implanted in the womb seven days after fertilization. Naturalists may try to call a child equal to any living plant or animal. These descriptions of human life are gross misconceptions. The Catholic Church on the other hand gives the sperm, the egg, the child in the womb, the one-year-old, the adult, the crippled, the aged (and the criminal) the dignity they deserve—that *all* human life is sacred from its beginning. How can you relate this important fact to your children?

_____

_____

_____

"'Before I formed you in the womb I knew you, and before you were born I consecrated you; I appointed you a prophet to the nations.'" (Jeremiah 1:5). The strong do not have dominion over the poor, the weak, and the defenseless. The Church was and always will be pro-life. God made us in his image. Our life is a gift of the Creator. Jesus redeemed us in the incarnation, passion, death, and resurrection; and offers us the supreme gift, the gift of eternal life. Explain that we are obligated to respect life and care for it even if it involves humiliation, suffering, and death.

_____

_____

_____

59. Realize beauty of natural family planning

On natural family planning, help young adults know that it is the only thing you would consider if you needed to space children. It is for *married* couples, and the only child spacing approved by the Church. The Church says NFP is moral when used for postponing pregnancy for serious and just reasons. These reasons must respect Church teachings: family structure, human dignity, the Sacrament of Marriage, and the good of society. Postponing pregnancy through NFP should never be used for mere convenience nor should it include anti-life secular techniques. Instead, we must discern God's will and always be open to parenthood. You might want to skip the rest of this part until they may need it in marriage, or until they need to teach it in the priesthood or religious life. Read it yourself and discuss with *teens* only the question at end.

If *adult* children need to know about NFP, tell them it helps married men and women avoid or achieve pregnancy by an awareness of the fertile time of the month. Designed by God, NFP is safe, moral, and simple to use. It is current. It developed into a fine science just as other forms of technology advanced in the last thirty years. Two NFP methods follow:

Creighton Model Fertility Care System (a manner of spacing children by teaching women about the biological parameters of their fertility):

* A review said the method is "over 99% effective in avoiding pregnancy...."[22] With accurate statistics such as this, we must be unselfish and open to life in accordance with God's will. "Thy hands fashioned and made me..." (Job 10:8). We are called to holiness. Costs are minimal and include classes, books, and charts.

Sympto-Thermal Method (a manner of spacing children by observing natural functions of the body, slightly different from above):

* Couple to Couple League reports, "NFP can be used at the 99% level of effectiveness by married couples..."[23] It is easy to learn and use, and is accurate even if woman has high incidence of vaginal infections. Costs are minimal and include classes or home study, books, charts, thermometer, and magazine.

Information on NFP is in the bibliography at end of this chapter. Also, ask a priest or doctor about NFP teachers. It can be used for both postponing as well as achieving pregnancy.

NFP users have an extremely low divorce rate, between one and five percent.[24] Spiritually, NFP if used unselfishly builds lasting marriages because couples are open to life and to the acceptance of children into their homes. NFP builds communication between husband and wife and makes family planning a shared responsibility. The periods of abstinence build excitement in marriage. The NFP couple enjoys a honeymoon each month.

Natural family planning can be a boon to families. Bob Ryder and Hubert Campbell proclaimed in *The Lancet*, "Whether one looks at it from the ecological, feminist, economic, family, or just plain common-sense point of view, all women [and men, too] are entitled to this simple and fundamental information."[25] NFP is safe, accurate, and economical. Little time and money is spent on doctor, pharmacy, and hospital visits because of complications, as one would have with unnatural forms of birth control.

NFP is moral when used for just reason, because married couples having intercourse in their fertile time do not block fertilization. NFP does not harm a man, woman, or child's body. NFP does not defy the will of God as artificial birth control does. It does not make women (men, too) objects to be used. It is not abortifacient as some unnatural methods. NFP methods, today, are superior to the old NFP rhythm methods. NFP is God's plan, and it is adaptable for today's married couple.

Because of the positive nature of NFP, will artificial birth control fall into the same oblivion as artificial fireplaces, plastic flowers, and the Model T? Probably not, although the average NFP family has about four children, many other couples are unjustly afraid of, or do not know of, natural methods of postponing pregnancy.

Studies show that an average married couple has intercourse about four to seven times per month. Therefore, the approximate ten-day abstinence of NFP during a woman's fertile time becomes a natural, feasible alternative to artificial birth control for the faint-hearted. Since NFP makes so much sense and is so natural, then why do you seldom hear it advertised? There may be other reasons, but the bottom line is that it makes little profit.

One way parents can turn the teen pregnancy, abortion, and divorce rates around is if parents use NFP for just reason. When they use NFP and abstain from the marital act for ten days a month, their teenagers get the powerful message that teens can surely refrain from sex until they get married. Conversely, condoms in wastepaper baskets and artificial birth control pills in the cupboard send another message to young people—"If Mom and Dad can do it, so can I." In the sexually saturated society we have today, it will take effective actions such as a small amount of abstinence from parents to turn the out-of-wedlock pregnancy rate and all its ramifications around.

After reading the above yourself, explain to young adults the accuracy, goodness, economy, safety, and morality of NFP, if needed in marriage for just and serious reasons.

---

60. Explain truth about contraception and abortifacients

You may want to discuss with young adults the dangerous effects of artificial birth control, and the teachings of the Church against it. It is not to be used by unmarried or married people. It is not unitive or procreative. It prevents fertilization and/or stops implantation of the newly formed child. A report of E. F. Jones and J. D. Forrest pronounced, "At any given time, three-quarters of adolescent women who have had sex are at risk of unintended pregnancy. Most at-risk teenagers use contraceptives."[26] This primes women for back-up abortion.

Young adults need to understand, for married people the differences between the goodness of NFP and the "evil" of artificial birth control as stated in the *Catechism of the Catholic Church*.[27] NFP is effective, medically safe, and when used unselfishly, marriage strengthening and moral. On the other hand, artificial birth control can be medically unsafe for men, women, and children. Further, it weakens marriages because it degrades women, leaves the father out of decision-making, and worse, it closes couples to God's gift of love and life.

Some may say, all child spacing is the same, whether it is NFP or artificial birth control. This is wrong. With NFP, we abstain during the fertile time and do nothing to damage the egg, sperm, or human embryo. However, when we use artificial birth control, we deliberately destroy the fertility process by using chemicals, devices, or surgery. These methods (1) prevent the ovum from developing, (2) or stop the sperm from fertilizing it, (3) or stop the human embryo (baby) from implanting in the womb by thinning the endometrial lining and causing a spontaneous abortion. Thus, artificial birth control attacks human nature, but NFP preserves human nature, the most precious God-given nature in the world. Explain this to young adults.

_____

_____

_____

_____

Discuss with them the fruits of the Holy Spirit: charity, joy, peace, patience, kindness, goodness, generosity, gentleness, faithfulness, modesty, self-control, and chastity. Tell young adults how artificial birth control says "*no*" to the "fruits…":

* No charity, because it erases spirituality,

* No joy, because it can cause death,

* No peace, because it wrecks your body,

* No patience, because it encourages abortion,

* No kindness, because it begets disrespect,

* No goodness, because it can ruin a baby's health,

* No generosity, because it attacks unborn life,

* No self-control, because it embraces self-love, and

* No chastity, because it assists fornication and adultery.

* No gentleness, because it can alter genetic inheritance,

* No faithfulness, because it escalates broken marriages,

* No modesty, because it bolsters out-of-wedlock birth.

"[H]e spilled the semen on the ground lest he should give offspring to his brother. And what he did was displeasing in the sight of the Lord, and he slew him also" (Genesis 38, 9-10). Artificial birth control for teens OR adults, married or not, is immoral.

Read this part (below) so that you, yourself, can understand the culture of death. It may be, however, too graphic for teens. You would not have to sample spoiled apples to develop a taste for good fruit. Teens do not have to be taught unnecessary details of illicit ways of regulating birth to understand and appreciate NFP from Exercise 59, above. Dwell mostly on the positive nature of NFP. However, the following information on some methods of artificial birth control is important to know yourself, in case someone in the family listened to the culture, and thinks that regulating birth in this way is the cure-all to sexually transmitted disease, teen pregnancy, and marital spacing of children. It is not. Now, after reading the text below yourself, assist teens with discussions at end of this exercise.

Condom

* The AIDS virus is smaller than semen; therefore, the failure rate in preventing AIDS is higher than the failure rate for preventing pregnancy. *Social Science and Medicine* said, "results of HIV transmission studies indicate that condoms may reduce risk of HIV infection by [only] approximately 69%."[28]

* Pregnancy failure rates of latex condoms when used by teenagers are between 13.2% and 27.3% based on poverty status.[29]

* *Family Resources Center News* reported,

> Thomas Fitch, M.D., a clinical professor of pediatrics at the University of Texas Health Science Center (San Antonio), presented conclusive evidence why condoms cannot stop the plague of STDs. There is no evidence that condoms are effective against human papilloma virus (HPV), the cause of genital warts. HPV may cause over 90% of all cervical cancer, which takes the lives of 8,000 American women annually. He reports that about 30% of American men and women have this virus.... Condoms similarly offer little protection

against syphilis or against herpes, an incurable virus infecting an esti-mated 30 million Americans.[30]

* The CCL Family Foundations magazine said:

> Women who used birth control methods [condoms, diaphragms, spermicides, and withdrawal] that prevented sperm and seminal fluids from reaching the uterus were more than twice as likely to develop preeclampsia.
>
> ...[It] is the third-ranking cause of pregnancy related death, follow-ing infection and hemorrhage. Preeclampsia can also retard the baby's development or kill the baby before birth.
>
> Preeclampsia usually causes hypertension and retention of fluids in tissues and cells, but in more severe cases, the pregnant woman may suffer kidney failure, convulsions, and death....[31]

Sterilization

* Peter Gott, M.D., relates it is "considered permanent." It is either "extremely difficult—or impossible—to reverse." It does not prevent "AIDS or other sexually transmitted diseases."[32]

* Barbara Seaman, founder of the National Women's Health Network said com-plications include:

> ...cardiac arrest, hemorrhage, severe infection, perforation or burn-ing of the intestines, and pulmonary embolism. Some women develop periods of depression....Fifteen percent say they regret the surgery....
>
> Nonetheless, sterilization of one or the other partner has become the most popular form of birth control for American couples past thirty...[33]

* According to Couple to Couple League:

> Dr. [H. J.] Roberts and others think that the effects [of sperm anti-bodies that develop in about 50% of patients] on a man's immune sys-tem cause a host of problems though they do not claim definitive proof....What Roberts and others have seen and think are (or may be) related to vasectomy: Thrombophlebitis, pulmonary embolism, infec-tion, arthopathy (arthritis), narcolepsy, multiple sclerosis, migraine and

related headaches, hypoglycemia, allergic manifestations, emotional disturbances, impaired sexual function, kidney stones, angina pectoris and heart attack, tumors and cancer.[34]

Intrauterine Device called IUD

* When a substance or device expels an embryonic person (baby), as in this case, it is called abortifacient. "A Guide to Methods of Birth Control" said, "IUDs are placed in the...[womb] and work by creating conditions which immobilize sperm, preventing them from fertilizing eggs. [IUDs] Can also create conditions inhospitable to eggs before and [to the human embryo] after fertilization..." It warns of "infection," "ectopic pregnancy," and "uterine perforation."[35] Almost all are off the United States market because of cost of manufacturer's liability.

* It does not prevent sexually transmitted diseases.

Combined Oral Artificial Birth Control Pill

* Risks and abortifacient qualities are reported by Population Crisis Committee in "A Guide to Methods of Birth Control": "Method may increase risk of stroke, heart attack, and blood clots," among other warnings. "A Guide..." also reports, three mechanisms of action: "Presence of estrogen and progestin suppresses ovulation, thickens cervical mucus to block passage of sperm and thins endometrial lining."[36] Thinning of the endometrial lining makes it difficult or impossible for a baby to implant. One study said that 85 percent of all abortions are chemical kind from artificial birth control methods such as the IUD and the pill. The rest (15%) are from surgical abortions.[37]

* Chris Kahlenborn, MD said, "An analysis in 1990 of the research up to that time...showed that women who used the [p]ill for 4 or more years before their first full-term pregnancy had a 72% increased risk of developing breast cancer."[38]

* The pill encourages teen sexual activity because they fear pregnancy less. At the same time, the pill decreases in effectiveness when taken improperly and in low doses. (Refer to Carol Everett's statement further in this exercise, on artificial birth control.)

* It may increase a woman's chances of getting sexually transmitted diseases. Preliminary studies showed large increases of AIDS infection in monkeys injected with progesterone. *USA Today* quoted researcher Preston Marx of the Aaron Diamond AIDS Research Center, New York, "Progesterone apparently caused thinning of protective vaginal tissue."[39]

* The Church says the pill (and other forms of artificial birth control) creates a *moral* problem that causes marriage breakups. Now, science finds that a woman who takes the pill creates a *physical* problem also affecting the breakup of their marriage, since she may no longer be attracted to her spouse because she took the pill. A report in *Nature* says a woman who takes the pill is attracted to a different male face preference than before using this chemical.[40] A somewhat similar report came from Swiss researchers.[41]

* Swiss researchers also said unmarried women taking the pill chose husbands with similar (as opposed to opposite) immune systems, which is unnatural; hence, they may produce children with weak immune systems.[42]

* *Scientific American* has grave concerns about xenoestrogens (certain types of foreign estrogens). These are in chlorinated organic compounds such as Chlordane, DDT and some PCBs; plastics; pharmaceuticals such as birth-control pills and estrogen-replacement therapies; and fuel constituents such as aromatic hydrocarbons. They report:

> [Aside from the speculation of breast cancer] analyses issued by the German, British and Danish governments have combined with earlier studies to suggest that xenoestrogen and other endocrine-disrupting materials are also harming men and wildlife....Indeed, it appears that such compounds may contribute to abnormal development in animals and to a range of reproductive disorders that have reportedly become increasingly common in men worldwide—notably testicular cancer, undescended testes, urinary tract defects and lowered sperm counts.[43]

* Barbara Seaman, author of *The Doctor's Case Against the Pill*, reported these problems with the pill: It causes a deficiency in "vitamins C, thiamine (B1), riboflavin (B2), pyridoxine (B6), B12, folic acid, and E..." and in turn may effect "birth defects." She also says, "modern research, published in England, shows that the suicide rate is tripled in [p]ill users. The chemicals in the [p]ill deplete vitamin B6, which in turn alters brain metabolism, leading to depression."[44]

* Dr. Ellen Grant worked at University College Hospital and the headquarters of the Family Planning Association in London studying a wide range of oral contraceptive pills. Results were printed in the *British Medical Journal* and the *Lancet*. In her book, *Sexual Chemistry*, she said:

Danish reproduction researchers checked back to 1938. Since then the quality of semen has declined so rapidly in pill-taking countries that the average man's sperm count has fallen by 50 percent....

Blood zinc levels are lowered by oestrogen, progestogens and testosterone....

Zinc deficiency contributes to dyslexia, learning problems, upper respiratory infections, hyperactivity and food allergies....

Professor [Jean] Jofen [a New York psychologist] had found that *the lower the child's IQ, the younger the mother had been when she was first introduced to hormones....*

If a mother is given oestrogens in early pregnancy, her XY genetically male baby can be born with female-type genitalia—the male is feminised. If the mother is given testosterone or a progestogen...her XX genetically female baby can be masculinised displaying dubious genitalia and a small penis at birth....

Our genetic inheritance has been protected, mixed, enriched but not altered more quickly than it can be repaired—never until now.[45]

Abortion Pill (Mifepristone, named Mifeprex® or RU-486)

* "A Guide to Methods of Birth Control" reports:

> RU-486 is the first anti-progestin drug approved specifically to induce menstruation and for very early pregnancy termination.
> Cramping, nausea, diarrhea may occur.
> Warning signs...fever, chills, muscle aches, fatigue, abdominal pain, tenderness to abdomen, heavy bleeding, vaginal discharge with strong odor, delayed resumption of menstruation (6 or more weeks).[46]

Plan B (so-called "morning-after pill" or "emergency contraception")

* A combination of chemicals work to alter the lining of the uterus so that a newly conceived baby cannot implant. Chemicals may have dangerous side effects for the mother, also.

<u>Anti-Beta HCG Vaccine</u> (an antibody that attacks the HCG hormone that sustains pregnancy, thus causing it to be abortifacient)

* William Corey reported in *CCL Family Foundations*, "Vials of tetanus toxoid containing [Beta] HCG have appeared in immunization programs in Mexico and the Philippines [without knowledge to the recipients]."[47]

Giving our young people (and their parents) artificial birth control is comparable to throwing gasoline into a fireplace. How big will the fire grow before we try to extinguish it? How much damage to humanity will it cause? How long will it take to alter us to the state of ashes?

Greg Schleppenbach, a state director of pro-life, reported a huge number of teens choose to be sexually active because of the promotion of unnatural forms of birth control. Further, when used by teens, it increases rather than decreases teen pregnancies.[48]

Carol Everett, a former abortion clinic manager, further explains the high teen pregnancy and abortion rate:

> We gave her a low dose [P]ill with a high rate of pregnancy, because we knew that her mother wouldn't nag her to take her birth control pill. She would forget it, and she would come back pregnant. We actually had an agenda, I'm sorry to say. It was three to five abortions out of every young woman between the ages of thirteen and eighteen…
> …we knew we could get them [for repeat abortions].[49]

From what you have just read, give a few good reasons why artificial birth control does not prevent the high teen pregnancy, sexually transmitted disease, and abortion rates we have today.

_____

_____

_____

_____

Pope Paul VI reaffirmed the Church's opposition to artificial birth control because it "is in contradiction with the design constitutive of marriage, and with the will of the Author of Life." It stands between "life" and "love", and "render[s] procreation impossible." Meanwhile, he said NFP used for "serious motives" by married couples is in harmony with the teachings of the Church.[50]

An executive director for Couple to Couple League for NFP said, 'More than 95% of young Catholic couples do not follow the Church's firm teaching that contraception is never permitted and is always objectively a mortal sin. This [teaching] isn't just a "whim" of the Church; it's God's plan for happy and healthy marriages and families.'[51] Parents must help young people understand.

Consider that *The Catechism of the Catholic Church* says you must follow your conscience, but you must strive to find out the path of Christ.[52] The path of Christ says artificial birth control and abortion, done with full knowledge and complete consent of the will, are mortal sins. Relate to young adults how this negates us from using contraceptives and abortifacients.

_____

_____

_____

_____

Pope Paul VI warned in *Of Human Life Humanae Vitae* that "Artificial birth control...[could easily] be opened up towards conjugal infidelity...lowering of morality...[loss of] respect for the woman...[and] government...solution of a family problem."[53] How many of these things do you see presently happening?

_____

_____

_____

Purchase a copy of Pope Paul VI's encyclical *Humanae Vitae* in the bibliography and discuss it with your children.

John and Sheila Kippley said:

> In the field of organized religion, 1930 was...a landmark year. In England, the bishops of the Anglican Church voted to allow the practice of contraception for cases of severe hardship. This was by no means a unanimous decision, and Anglican Bishop Gore warned against other moral consequences that would result.[54]

He was right. Some moral consequences that resulted were abortion, euthanasia, in vitro fertilization, cloning, embryo experiments, test tube reproductions, and surrogate motherhood. Explain both statements above to young adults, and develop a prayer for the ban on harmful artificial birth control that inflames sexual immorality. Include the cardinal virtues of prudence, justice, fortitude, and temperance in your prayer.

_____

_____

_____

_____

Again, there is a significant contrast between having intercourse while blocking or aborting fertilization (artificial birth control) and not having intercourse during one's fertile time (natural family planning). Artificial birth control kills the life process of the baby through pills, plugs, devices, and surgeries. This is not love and it is not life. Conversely, NFP lets you enjoy a baby when the time is right. (That means married couples may use NFP to space their babies for just and serious physical, psychological, social, and economic conditions.) You might tell young adults that practicing NFP is similar to receiving a basket of eggs from a kindly old lady, thanking her for them, and then keeping them cool until the couple can enjoy them. However, practicing artificial birth control compares to receiving the basket of eggs, leaving them on the doorstep to rot, and then asking for more when the time seems right. The little old lady just may say to the latter, "'I never knew you...'" (Matthew 7:23)! How would you explain the physical and spiritual differences between artificial birth control and NFP to young adults?

_____

_____

_____

You will not want to leave this important information up to the local pre-marriage programs. Without a parent's backup, there is little the Church can do but teach the sexuality issues into one ear as they go out the other. Your children deserve to know this critical information before secular culture sets their minds. Waiting until they are twenty-five is too late.

61. Explain more truth about abortion

Abortion might seem a good choice to teenagers until they consider the facts about it, just as opium might seem a good choice until you find out how much spiritual and physical damage it does. To make rational decisions about abortion, young people need to understand four things:

Unborn child

The development of the unborn child—Frontline Publishing explains it this way:

* First day, "egg is fertilized by sperm…"
* Third week, "brain, spinal cord, and nervous system develop."
* Fourth week, "heart begins to beat."
* Fifth week, "Arms with hands & fingers, legs with feet & toes, and eyes can be seen."[55]

Whatever the stage of the unborn child, he or she is still a creation and image of God.

Effects on child

Here are the inhumane surgical abortion methods used by abortionists as Frontlines states (determine if your child can handle the gruesome details):

* Suction Aspiration used before 14 weeks of pregnancy: "suction machine…is used to pull the placenta and fetus into parts small enough to pass out of your body through the suction tube."
* Dilation and Curettage used before the first 14 weeks of pregnancy: "looped-shaped knife…[scrapes baby from] the wall of your…womb]."
* Dilation and Evacuation after 14 weeks of pregnancy: "medical instrument resembling pliers…pull[s] the fetus into smaller parts and removes those parts from your body through the cervix."
* Dilation and Extraction "Partial Birth" after 22 weeks of pregnancy: abortionist "uses large forceps to grasp a leg, and pull it down into the vagina. After the body is delivered, the skull is lodged at the cervical opening. The…[abortionist] makes an incision in the base of the fetal skull…and empties the contents of the baby's skull."[56]

Whatever the reason for abortion, the unborn child was the victim: The healthy child became debilitated. The handicapped child suffered discrimination. The unwanted child acquired no adoption. The poor child suffered ultimate poverty. The child of pro-choice had no choice. The child of rape suffered more abuse; and worse, the child of God died. The Bible, though, protects children. It says, God "blesses" the child "within you." (Psalm 147:13)

Effects on mother

A few of the dire effects of abortion on the mother:

* David Reardon of the Elliot Institute for Social Sciences Research reviewed over twenty-six studies from the Association of Interdisciplinary Research relating to abortion and said:

> [Post-abortion] women are more likely to engage in drug and alcohol abuse...
> [T]eenagers who have one abortion are four times more likely to have a subsequent abortion...
> Women who have had abortions are more likely to subsequently require welfare assistance,...
> Women who have had repeat abortions tend to have an increasing number of health problems and greater personality disintegration,...
> Post-abortion women have greater difficulty establishing permanent relationships with a male partner. They are more likely to never marry, more likely to divorce, and more likely to go through a long string of unsuccessful relationships. This inability to form a nuclear family reduces household income and increases the probability that the woman and her children will require public assistance.
> Women who have had repeat abortions are more likely to desire children and are likely to carry one or more subsequent replacement pregnancies to term....[57]

* *CCL Family Foundations* reports:

> [Researchers] found that women age 45 or younger who had had an induced abortion ran a 50% higher risk of developing breast cancer than women in the same age group who had been pregnant at least once but had not obtained an abortion.... In addition, a completed pregnancy did not protect women from this elevated risk.[58]

Whatever the reason for abortion, the mother is the victim of unnecessary surgery and tremendous physical, emotional, spiritual, economic, or social strain.

Even when she and the child are in danger of death, all conventional measures and rational attempts should be used to safeguard the lives of each.

Death proponents

The inconsistencies of the abortion movement:

* Abortionists say women should have the right to choose, but "right to choose" takes on a whole new meaning if one dares to complete their statement and say, "Right to choose destruction of life." Some may even say they are personally opposed to abortion, but they support the right to choose. There is, however, no common ground on abortion. You are either for abortion or you are against abortion.

* Abortionists try to tell us that getting rid of the baby puts one's life back to normal, but nothing is further from the truth. Abortion, even in the cases of rape and incest, causes lasting grief. Conversely, the choices of either keeping the baby, or finding loving, adoptive parents gives one dignity, healing, health, and sanity.

* The abortion movement declares equal rights among men and women. If the abortion movement, though, really wants equal rights among the sexes, *both* men and women would also share equal responsibilities. That is, men as well as women would support the child physically and monetarily until adulthood. On the other hand, the abortion groups ambiguously advocate less of women than of men, because women can abort, but men have to support the child. What the abortion people are really saying is that women are irresponsible, weak, and inferior to men; which, of course, is not true.

* Abortion groups say life worsens when abortion is illegal. On the contrary, American Life League said nearly five hundred doctors signed a declaration that reads:

> I agree that there is never a situation…where a preborn child's life need be intentionally destroyed by procured abortion for the purpose of saving the life of the mother.[59]

If surgical abortion is not necessary, then all human life becomes better without abortion. First, ex-abortionists finally following the medical ethics of their Hippocratic Oath can save lives rather than kill them. Second, unmarried couples won't rely on abortion as another form of birth control. Third, there is proven testimony that without government support of matters such as abortion, the public also gradually ceases to support it. Without abortion supporters, the "life worsens" theory will quickly revert into the "all life is sacred" theory.

* Surgical and chemical abortion advocates revel in lucrative secularism and praise for eliminating unwanted children; whereas childless couples wait on long lists to adopt.

* Abortionists, in our upside-down-world (where bad is good and good is bad), are made to look good. Other scandals are bad; however, abortionists tip the scales in their evil child killings.

* Abortionists say we need abortion (artificial birth control and euthanasia, too) to curb world population growth. Numerous populations have declined, though, and are expected to decline further in coming years. Thus, we need more children, and we need them in two-parent families. We need children to grow and care for the increasing older population. We need children as future leaders to care for the increasing number of children born out-of-wedlock, perhaps destined to poverty unless they have help.

Whatever the reason for abortion, the whole country suffers. Mother Teresa once said, "Any country that accepts abortion is not teaching its people to love but to use any violence to get what they want. This is why the greatest destroyer of love and peace is abortion…"

The following text is based on *Evangelium Vitae* and written by Richard M. Doerflinger, Secretariat for Pro-life Activities, of the now United States Conference of Catholic Bishops:

> The Holy Father sets out a powerful intellectual case on the need to respect all human life, regardless of its age or condition. He points out that life is our first and greatest gift from God, on which every other gift and every other right depend. If we fail to respect and protect this gift for everyone, we will descend into a bottomless abyss of discrimination, in which the strong make self-serving decisions about whether the weak deserve to live.[60]

How could you discuss with your children the statements of Mother Teresa and Richard M. Doerflinger?

_____

_____

_____

_____

At what age should your children know about the development of the unborn child?_____...about the types of abortion and its effects on mother and child?_____...about the inconsistencies of the abortion movement?_____...about the Church's stand on human life?_____...about your expectations?_____

Inform your teenage children of the forty million surgical abortions tragically performed since 1973 in the United States, since the <u>Roe vs. Wade</u> decision, plus millions of other chemical abortions. The *Catechism of the Catholic Church* says, "Human life must be respected and protected absolutely from the moment of conception [fertilization]...."[61] Children are gifts from God, not choices. Children are assets to families, not liabilities.

One reason girls give for having abortions is that they did not want others to know they had sex and were expecting. Let your children know you would support them in the tough times such as an out-of-wedlock pregnancy.

Assure your teenagers that if out-of-wedlock pregnancy happened in their lives, you would love your grandchild and you would work it through. The fetus is a live child from the moment of conception, and abortion would not be an option because it kills sacred life. You would not like what they had done (acted promiscuously), but you would still love them the same and you would want your grandchild to live.

If you have an unmarried expectant daughter or son in your house, she or he needs:

* To have immediate physical and emotional support from family and friends. An expectant son or daughter needs hugs and help. It is too late for sermons. (After physical and emotional needs have been met, though, you will want to lovingly review lifestyle changes.)

* To allow God to work through the gift he has given.

* To know about the help and understanding in the community that includes ministers, Christian crisis pregnancy centers, religious charities, Catholic social services, homes for the unwed, and adoption agencies.

* To know that being a parent is a wonderful vocation and that one's future isn't in jeopardy because of it.

* To find realistic long-term spiritual and physical goals for oneself and the baby.

* To know that adoption places children into loving arms, and it is a considerate thing to do for both the baby and the adoptive parents.

Relate information if you can, of a woman who aborted her baby. Would the child be alive today if the mother had had a good support system?

_____

_____

_____

_____

Let your children know that in spite of all their Christian education against abortion, many times young people make mistakes and abort anyway. They think it is an easy way to avoid the stress of school, work, awards, parental expectations, and desolation. Tell them you *never* want them to choose this monstrosity, and you will help them keep the precious baby. On the contrary and to your dismay, tell them if they have *completely* defiled God's will (and yours) and aborted a child, you hope they learned something by their mistakes, went to confession to clear their conscience, told God and their child they were sorry, and made amends. Explain how they will regret the abortion, and they must begin to follow Jesus and pray and do good for others. They can become staunch defenders of the right-to-life. It takes months or years to heal, but it can happen with the peace and the grace of God. God's mercy and love are awesome and limitless. (For help in crisis pregnancy, go to the bibliography at the end of this chapter.)

62. Explain euthanasia

The euthanasia movement builds off the abortion movement. The abortion movement builds off the contraceptive movement. They all build off the culture of death. The euthanasia movement (promoters of assisted suicide) reinforces self-destruction. Jack Kevorkian, infamous for assisting suicides, said: "'The voluntary self elimination of individual and mortally diseased or crippled lives can only enhance the preservation of public health and welfare.'"[62] This movement wrongly promotes the theories that pain and mental anguish are unbearable and cannot be controlled, and it encourages people to kill themselves.

Here are some Christian facts negating the euthanasia movement:

* Believing in the fifth Commandment, "Thou shalt not kill." God has a purpose for all human beings. Our fate is God's decision, not ours.

* Believing in the sanctity of all human life. Mercy killing won't preserve public health and welfare as suicide supporters declare. More likely, mercy killing makes the poor and disabled fearful that they stand next in line for annihilation.

* Acting to distribute highly sophisticated pain relief to trained health care providers in remote areas. This planet already has adequate pain relieving medicines. The problems are distribution and training, and not lack of supply.

* Understanding that all people have value, dignity, and worth. The weak and infirm must not be treated shamefully because they need assistance. They should not be made to feel that suicide and euthanasia are "courtesies" one does for family. Be cautious of end-of-life contracts, sign only Catholic directives instead of living wills, and then double-check with the Secretariat for Pro-life Activities (listed in the bibliography) or your Catholic state pro-life director.

The evils of the culture of death will not triumph if we instill truth in children. Teaching chastity, natural family planning, and other pro-life issues brings peace, respect, grace, togetherness, health, life, joy, and love. The results of promiscuity, artificial birth control, abortion, euthanasia, and such, however, are hostility, disrespect, depravity, division, sickness, hatred, and physical and spiritual death (hell). How would you share this with a teen?

_____

_____

_____

_____

Note: Teaching our children about Christian sexual morals is rewarding. If the negative effects of the secular sexual movement are real for our young people as stated in this chapter, then let us teach our children about the responsible decisions of chastity and Christian marriage.

Why teach them irresponsible ways to control their bodies (and those of the unborn)? Responsible decisions for young adults are *not*: "If I have homosexual tendencies, I should choose sodomy as a lifestyle." "If I just take the pill, I will not get pregnant." "If I use a condom, I may not contact a sexually transmitted disease." "If I have an abortion, everything will be all right." "If I want to end my life, that's all right, too." On the contrary, responsible choice means:

I know why God chose the monogamous heterosexual marriage relationship and moral Christian values for us. I will, therefore, not choose sex outside of marriage, artificial birth control, abortion, or suicide as my lifestyle. Then, I can increase my chances of having a better future that protects my off-spring from being unwanted; prevents my family-to-be and me from getting sexually transmitted diseases; keeps us in a safe loving home; and shields my marriage and my family from distrust, divorce, death, spiritual poverty, and the possibility of hell.

Some would say that teen childbearing (with all due respect to unmarried moms who carry their pregnancies to term) is the result of our culture's social problems—welfare dependence, drug and alcohol abuse, crime, and the school dropout rate. If true, then we should go one step back and declare that not single moms, but those who profit by (and encourage) the sale of sex, artificial birth control, abortion, and euthanasia to our young (and old) people have become cause and symptom of most of America's social ills!

If our social and physical ills result from those who lure our young people into single parent households, let's take a second look at teenage promiscuity and at its luring relationship with unnatural birth control and abortion encouraged from the adult world. Chastity and purity for our young (and old) people—not secular sex education, artificial birth control centers, abortion industries, and the culture of death—are the ways we will climb out of welfare dependence, drug and alcohol abuse, crime, and the school dropout rate. That is why this chapter is one of the largest. Spend quality and quantity time on it with your teenage children.

We, as parents, can offer young people decision-making talents that will not ruin their lives and the lives of their unborn—our precious next generation. Now is our chance to be the expert, teaching chaste living to our children with the help of Jesus and his Church.

We must control ourselves through faith. On the other hand, following the wrong resources gets us into trouble. Sexual abuse is a confusing subject to children. Parents must not only speak the truth about it to them, but parents must speak out to all of society, also, and say enough is enough. We don't want it on our television. We don't want it in our government. We don't want it on our doorstep. Apologize to your children. Tell them your generation and a couple of generations past didn't do a good job in fighting sexual misconduct. Ask them to do better with God's help.

In the next chapter, there may be no depression and violence in your family life; though, it would be hard to find the perfect home. In any case, you will benefit by alerting your teenagers to help others in need.

Endnotes:

1. *Catechism of the Catholic Church* (Washington, D.C.: United States Catholic Conference, 1997), Publication no. 5-110, #2348, p. 564.

2. Ibid., #2346, 2396, 2399 & 2400, p. 563.

3. Pontifical Council for the Family, *The Truth and Meaning of Human Sexuality* (Massachusetts: Pauline Books & Media, 1996), p. 28.

4. Reverend Mark Watkins, *Fostering Vocations in Your Family*, audio tape (Covina, CA: St. Joseph Communications, n.d.)

5. Michael McManus, "How to Avoid a Bad Marriage," ed. Donald E. Wildmon, *AFA Journal* (July 1993): p. 21.

6. Jenna Zark, "Date Rape, What You Need To Know," *Scholastic Choices Magazine* (Feb. 1990): pp. 7, 10.

7. National Victims' Center—now called National Center for Victims of Crime, cited March 30, 2004 in "Rape Facts and Prevention, About Rape—Myths and Facts," report prepared by Department of Student Health, Office of Health Promotion, University of Virginia, Web site: www.geocities.com/john1234567891311/. (n.d.).

8. "Rethinking the Rites of Passage: Alcohol Abuse on America's College and University Campuses" executive summary for the Center on Addiction and Substance Abuse at Columbia University, New York (1993): p. 3.

9. Zark, op. cit., p. 10.

10. Rev. Robert J. Fox, *Charity, Morality, Sex, and Young People* (Virginia: Trinity Communications, 1987), pp. 81,79.

11. *Getting Smart About Sexually Transmitted Diseases* (Chicago, IL: G.D. Searle & Co., 1991), p. 4.

12. *The Other Epidemic...Chlamydia*, pamphlet by Parke-Davis (Warner-Lambert Company: 1988), p. 3,4,6.

13. Center for Disease Control and Prevention report, Web site: www.cdc.gov/std/Gonorrhea/STDFact-gonorrhea.htm. (2004): p. 2, 3.

14. *Getting Smart About Sexually Transmitted Diseases,* op. cit., p. 8.

15. Ibid., pp. 21-23.

16. "STD Sexually Transmitted Diseases," pamphlet (Planned Parenthood, Alameda/San Francisco, 1985).

17. *Getting Smart About Sexually Transmitted Diseases,* op. cit., pp. 30, 31.

18. "What You Should Know About AIDS" pamphlet (U.S. Public Health Service Centers for Disease Control, n.d.): p. 3.

19. Center for Disease Control, data 2003, Web site: cdc.gov/hiv/stats.htm#international (Feb. 25, 2004).

20. *Holy Hour of Reparation* booklet (Oak Lawn, IL: CMJ Marian Publishers/Soul Assurance, 2001), p. 13.

21. John Paul II, *The Splendor of Truth* (MA: St. Paul Books and Media, 1999), p. 45.

22. "Fertility Appreciation" pamphlet (Pope Paul VI Institute, Omaha, NE, n.d.) n.p.

23. John and Sheila Kippley, *Art of Natural Family Planning,* Fourth Edition (Cincinnati: Couple to Couple League, 1999), p. 139.

24. Kippley, op, cit., p. 245.

25. Bob Ryder and Hubert Campbell, "Natural Family Planning in the 1990s," *The Lancet,* Vol. 346, 7/22/95: pp.233-234 as cited by Judie Brown, "Natural Family Planning," *Communiqué* (25 Aug. 1995): p. 5.

26. E.F. Jones and J.D Forrest, "Contraceptive Failure Rates Based on the 1988 NSFG," Family Planning Perspectives, 24:12-19, 1992, Table 2, p. 15, 1984-1987 survey, cited in *Sex and America's Teenagers* (New York: The Alan Guttmacher Institute, 1994), p. 37.

27. *Catechism of the Catholic Church,* op. cit., #2370, p. 570.

28. Susan C. Weller, "A Meta-Analysis of Condom Effectiveness in Reducing Sexually Transmitted HIV," *Social Science and Medicine,* Vol. 36, #12, 6/93: p. 1635.

29. 1988 National Survey of Family Growth, cited by Elise F. Jones and Jacqueline Darroch Forrest, "Contraceptive Failure Rates Based on the 1988 NSFG," *Family Planning Perspectives,* vol. 24, No. 1 Jan./Feb. 1992: p. 15.

30. "Science and Faith: In Partnership For An STD-Free America," reprinted from *Life Insight,* September 1997, *Family Resources Center News,* Peoria, IL (January 1998): p.23.

31. University of North Carolina at Chapel Hill research published their findings in the *Journal of the American Medical Association* and *The Washington Post* (8 Dec. 1989); cited in *CCL Family Foundations* magazine, Couple to Couple League (Jan.-Feb. 1990): p. 3.

32. Peter Gott, M.D., "Health Report," #33, P.O. Box 91369, Cleveland, OH 44101-3369.

33. Barbara Seaman, *The Doctors Case Against the Pill* (Garden City, New York: Doubleday & Company, Inc., 1980), p. 185.

34. *H. J. Roberts, Is Vasectomy Worth the Risk? A Physician's case Against Vasectomania* (West Palm Beach: Sunshine Sentinal Press, 1993): 53-72, cited in *Art of Natural Family Planning*, op. cit., p. 17.

35. "A Guide to Methods of Birth Control" poster (Washington, D.C: Population Crisis Committee, n.d.)

36. Ibid.

37. "Test your knowledge of Birth Control in America," report by Protestants Against Birth Control, Milwaukee, as cited in *Celebrate Life* magazine, ed. Judie Brown, American Life League (May/June 1996): p. 30.

38. Romieu I, Berlin J, et al. "Oral contraceptives and breast cancer, Review and meta-analysis," *Cancer.* 1990: 66: 2253-2263; as cited by Chris Kahlenborn, M.D., "Breast Cancer Risk from The Pill" pamphlet (Dayton, Ohio: One More Soul, 2000), n.p.

39. "AIDS and Birth Control," USA Today (7 May, 1996), p. 1, as cited in *Communiqué* (31 May, 96): p. 1.

40. Studies from School of Psychology, University of St. Andrews; Hasegawa Laboratory, Department of Life Sciences, University of Tokyo; School of Life Sciences, Roehampton Institute London, Whitelands College, cited in "Menstrual Cycle Alters Face Preference," *Nature* Vol. 399, www.nature.com (24 June, 1999): p. 741.

41. *Proceedings of the Royal Society of London*, as cited by Steve Mirsky, "The Noses Have It" *Scientific American* (November, 1995): p. 20.

42. Ibid.

43. Devra Lee Davis and H. Leon Bradlow, "Can Environmental Estrogens Cause Breast Cancer?" *Scientific American* (Oct. 1995): pp. 166-169.

44. Seaman, op. cit., p. 16, 147.

45. Dr. Ellen Grant, MB ChB, DObstRCOG, *Sexual Chemistry* (Great Britain: Cedar, 1994), p. 4,13,12,35,261,27,37.

46. "A Guide to Methods of Birth Control," loc. cit.

47. William N. Corey, "Tetanus Vaccine Being Linked Future Abortions," *CCL Family Foundations*, The Couple to Couple League (Sep./Oct. 95): p. 12.

48. Greg Schleppenbach, State Director, Bishops' Pastoral Plan for Pro-Life Activities, "Safe Sex Abets Promiscuity," *West Nebraska Register* (25 Sep. 1992): p. 6.

49. John A. Thompson, Jr., "A Battle of Conscience" interview with Carole Everett, *University Review of Texas*, (February 1991), reprinted in *AFA Journal* (May 1991): pp. 20,21.

50. Paul VI, *Of Human Life, Humanae Vitae* (Massachusetts: St. Paul Books and Media, 1968), #13, #14, and #16.

51. E. William Sockey, III, Executive Director, Couple to Couple League Newsletter, Lent 2003, Couple to Couple League, Cincinnati.

52. *Cathechism of the Catholic Church*, op. cit., #1790-94, p.441.

53. Encyclical Letter of Paul VI, op. cit., #17.

54. John and Sheila Kippley, *Art of Natural Family Planning*, Fourth Edition (Cincinnati: Couple to Couple League, 1991), p. 40.

55. *Making an Informed Decision About Your Pregnancy*, pamphlet (Grand Rapids, Michigan 49548: Frontline Publishing, 2000), p. 2.

56. Ibid., p. 3.

57. Thomas Strahon, Association of Interdisciplinary Research studies, as cited by David Reardon, "Abortion and the Feminization of Poverty," *ALL About Issues* [Stafford, VA 22555] (Nov.-Dec. 1992): p. 26.

58. Research by Janet R. Daling of the Fred Hutchinson Cancer Research Center in Seattle and colleagues published in *Journal of the National Cancer Institute*, 2 Nov. 1994, cited by John F. Kippley in *CCL Family Foundations*, January-February 1995, pp. 2,7.

59. Judie Brown, "Doctors agree abortion is never necessary," *ALL NEWS* [Stafford, VA 22555] Vol. 10 No. 3, (March 2004): p. 4.

60. Richard M. Doerflinger, associate director for policy development, NCCB Secretariat for Pro-life Activities, "The Quality of Life: Who's to Judge?" report, *Respect Life*, National Conference of Catholic Bishops, Washington, DC 20017-1194 (1996)

61. *Cathechism of the Catholic Church*, op. cit., cf. CDF, Donum Vitae I,1., #2270, p.547.

62. Jack Kevorkian, Oakland County Circuit Court, 1990, cited in *HLI Reports*, newsletter 14:10, Human Life International, Front Royal, VA 22630 (Oct, 1996): p. 14.

Bibliography:

Adams, Jason T. *Called to Give Life*. Dayton, Oh 45405: One More Soul, 1846 N. Main Street, Telephone: 1-800-307-7685, 2003.

American Academy of Natural Family Planning (AANFP). St. Louis, Missouri 63141: 615 South New Ballas Road. Telephone 1-314-569-6495.

American Life League, gives pro-life information. Telephone: 1-540-659-4171, E-mail: jbrown@all.org. Web site: www.all.org.

American Life League Pregnancy Helpline. 1-800-67-BABY-6.

Billings Ovulation Method Association USA. ST. Paul, MN 55116: P.O. Box 16206.

Bower, Keith, ed-in-chief, and Judy J. Harris, ed. *New Corinthian's Curriculum*, grades K-8 sexuality education. Cincinnati, OH 45211: Foundation for the Family, P.O. Box 111184, Telephone: 513-471-2000, Web site: www.ccli.org, 1997.

Brown, Judie, ed. *Celebrate Life*, pro-life magazine. Stafford, VA 22555: American Life League, Inc. P.O. Box 1350, Telephone: 1-540-659-4171, Web site: www.all.org.

Catholic Singles, provides single Catholics with a way to meet friends or a spouse, or discern their religious vocation. Web site: www.StRaphael.net.

Catholic Social Services. Telephone: 1-800-CARE-002.

Center for Life Principles, resources for high school outreach. Telephone 1-425-883-8024, Web site: www.lifeprinciples.net.

Clowes, Brian, PhD. *The Facts of Life.* Front Royal, VA: Human Life International, 1997.

Couple to Couple League, teaches Sympto-Thermal method of natural family planning. Classes with teachers or home study. Cincinnati, OH 45211: Couple to Couple League, P.O. Box 111184, Telephone: 513-471-2000, (orders only) call 1-800-745-8252, Fax: 513-557-2449, Web site: www.ccli.org.

Courage/Encourage, Church approved group enables homosexual to live a chaste life. Web site: www.NYCourage@aol.com.

Daub, Elizabeth. *Reality Check,* pro-life youth publication. Stafford, VA 22555: American Life League, Inc., P.O. Box 1350, Telephone: 1-540-659-4171, Web site: www.rcheck@all.org.

Euteneuer, Rev. Thomas, President. *HLI Reports.* Front Royal, VA 22630: Human Life International, 4 Family Life, Telephone: 1-540-635-7884, Web site: www.hli.org.

Gift Foundation, The, helps you to be an effective "Apostle of Chastity" sharing the true meaning of marriage and chastity. Carpentersville, IL 60110: P.O. Box 95.

Gift of Love, helps homeless AIDS patients. New York, NY 10014: 657 Washington Street, Telephone: 718-292-0019.

Grant, Dr. Ellen, MB ChB, DObstRCOG. *Sexual Chemistry.* Great Britain: Cedar Publishing, 1994.

Harvey, John F., O.S.F.S. *The Truth About Homosexuality.* San Francisco, CA: Ignatius Press, 1996.

Hayes, Rev. Edward J., Rev. Msgr. Paul J. Hayes, Dorothy Ellen Kelly, R.N., and James J. Drummey. *Catholicism and Ethics*, a medical moral handbook. Norwood MA: C.R. Publications, Inc., 345 Prospect Street, Norwood, MA 02062, 1997.

Holy Hour of Reparation, booklet. Oak Lawn, IL 60454: CMJ Marian Publishers/Soul Assurance, P.O. Box 661. Telephone 888-636-6799.

John Paul II. *On The Family Familiaris Consortio*. MA: St. Paul Books & Media, 1982.

Kippley, John and Sheila. *Art of Natural Family Planning*. Cincinnati, OH 45211: Couple to Couple League, P.O. Box 111184, Telephone: 513-471-2000, (orders only) 800-745-8252, Fax: 513-557-2449, Web site: www.ccli.org.

Kippley, John F. "The Legacy of Margaret Sanger," pamphlet. Cincinnati, OH 45211: Couple to Couple League, P.O. Box 111184, Telephone: 513-471-2000, (orders only) 800-745-8252, Fax: 513-557-2449, Web site: www.ccli.org, 1988.

Lenahan, Philip. *Financial Foundations for the Family*. Temecula, CA 92589-0998: P.O. Box 890998, Telephone: 909-699-7066.

Marx, Rev. Paul, OSB. *Faithful for Life*. Front Royal, VA 22630: Human Life International, 4 Family Life, 1997.

Militello, Louis J. *Please Let Me Be Born*. Fenton, MO 63026: 1564 Fentcorp Drive, Telephone: 800-325-9414, 2001.

Mothers At Home. Telephone: 1-800-783-4MOM. Web site: www.mah.org.

National Association of At-Home Mothers. Web site: www.athomemothers.com.

Natural Family Planning Talks for Clergy, audio tapes to help anyone, especially priests to spread the pro-life NFP message. Ohio: One More Soul, Telephone: 1-800-307-7685.

One More Soul, non-profit apostolate dedicated to spread truth about the harm of artificial birth control and the blessing of children: includes information on pro-life doctors, NFP, and sterilization reversal. Dayton, Ohio 45406: One More Soul, 616 Five Oaks Avenue, Telephone: 1-800-307-7685, local 937-279-5433, Sterilization Reversal Hotline 612-755-7706, Web site: www.OMSoul.com.

Patron Saints Index, details, pictures, and prayer. Web site: www.catholic-forum.com/saints/indexsnt.htm.

Paul VI. *Of Human Life Humanae Vitae*. Boston: Pauline Books and Media, 1968.

Pharmacists For Life International. Powell, OH 43065-1281: P.O. Box 1281, 1-800-227-8359, E-mail: pfli@pfli.org.

Pope Paul VI Institute Creighton Model Fertility Care System, NaProEducation Technology (includes NFP). Omaha, NE 68106: 6901 Mercy Road, Telephone: 402-390-6600.

Pontifical Council on the Family. *The Truth and Meaning of Human Sexuality.* MA: Pauline Books & Media, 1996.

Project Rachel, National office for post-abortion reconciliation and healing. Telephone: 1-800-829-3477, Web site: www.marguette.edu/rachel.

Rachel's Vineyard, post-abortion help. Telephone: 1-877-HOPE-4-ME, Web site: www.rachelsvineyard.org.

Reardon, David C. *Making Abortion Rare.* Illinois: Acorn Books, 1996.

Secretariat for Pro-life Activities. Washington, D.C. 20017-1194: National Conference of Catholic Bishops, 3211 Fourth St. N E., Telephone: 1-202-541-3070, Fax: 1-202-541-3054.

Shannon, Marilyn. *Fertility, Cycles and Nutrition,* how your diet affects your menstrual cycles and fertility. Cincinnati, OH 45211: Couple to Couple League, P.O. Box 111184, Telephone: 513-471-2000, (orders only) call 1-800-745-8252, Fax: 513-557-2449, Web site: www.ccli.org, 2001.

Smith, Janet E. *Contraception Why Not?,* video or cassette. Dayton, OH 55406: One More Soul, 616 Five Oakes Avenue, Telephone: 1-800-307-SOUL (7685), 1994.

Szymkowiak, Ed. *The Ryan Report,* publication to stop Planned Parenthood. Stafford, VA 22555: STOPP International—a division of American Life League, Inc. P.O. Box 1350, Telephone: 1-540-659-4171, Web site: www.stoppinternational.org.

Vocations Congress, presents weekend retreats on vocations. Web site: www.vocations.com.

West, Christopher. *Good News About Sex and Marriage.* Ann Arbor: Servant Publications, 2000.

Wilson, Mercedes Arzu. *Love and Family.* San Francisco: Ignatius, 1996.

World Youth Alliance, pro-life international ecumenical, and interreligious network of young activists. Web site: www.worldyouthalliance.org.

Wood, Steve. *ABC's of Choosing a Good Husband* and *ABC's of Choosing a Good Wife*. Port Charlotte, FL 33952: Family Life Center, Dept. 0503cgw, 22226 Westchester Blvd., Telephone: 1-941-764-7725, Web site: www.dads.org, 2001 and 2003.

```
    1 God
  + 1 Mom and/or Dad
  + Purity
  - Violence
  ─────────────────
  = 1 Happy Family
```

Teach children gentle, positive, and Christian attitudes against violence. St. Thomas Aquinas said, "Impurity leads inevitably to violence."

Chapter VI

Avoid Violence

The *Catechism of the Catholic Church* says, "Everyone is responsible for his life before God who has given it to him. It is God who remains the sovereign Master of life. We are obliged to accept life gratefully and preserve it for his honor and the salvation of our souls...."[1]

Crime and violence invade every newscast. You wish your children could escape even the thought of it. Will it happen to your children? Who can say? In the back of your mind, a gnawing feeling cries out: "Because of the frightful statistics I constantly hear, my children should know how to prevent violent activities from gaining a stronghold in their lives."

The next pages help you teach your children gentle, positive, and Christian attitudes against violence. For example, until your children learned that ovens and toasters were hot, you constantly watched them. The question is: Do you want to watch your children forever so that they won't get burnt on destructive behavior, or do you want to inform them about the dangers on the streets and elsewhere so that as they enter adulthood, they can avoid the heat and protect themselves?

Some would say that talking about violence and such gives children the wrong ideas. Yet, did children ever get the wrong ideas when told band saws aren't toys? Did they get the wrong ideas when told matches burn fingers? Did they get the wrong ideas when told speeding causes accidents? It is better to have an alert child than an injured, naive one.

Equip yourself, now, to help your wide-eyed youngsters protect themselves from depression, suicide, delinquency, and gangs. "Surely goodness and mercy shall follow me all the days of my life..." (Psalm 23[22]:6).

(Again, as you speak with your children, follow instructions from the Introduction on the suitable age for each child.)

Depression and Suicide

Depressed and suicidal children mimic pressure cookers ready to explode. If we don't adjust the steam and heat—and when all else fails—if we don't summon a fix-it-man, then the cooker may very well explode. Our children's lives could blow out of control, too, if their situation isn't adjusted and they haven't found the proper fix-it-man.

Depressed and suicidal children have needs. They need to know how to let out steam; they need to know how to adjust their heated emotional problems; and if that doesn't work, they need help, from the fix-it-man, from someone, from anyone, but they need help.

Depression can become apparent in children of any age. Some types of depression might call for chemical intervention by a qualified bio-psychiatrist. Parents need to be able to identify: (1) normal adolescent mood swings—being happy then sad, sulky and gloomy; (2) spiritual warfare—sins of presumption, hopelessness, and despair; (3) mental illness—a disturbance of the mind that causes one to be emotionally upset. This section benefits children with normal and spiritual adolescent depressions. You will need extra help, however, with a child's mental depressions.

Help your children find happiness. Children want to be happy, not sad; it's part of their very nature. If depression and suicide doesn't seem to be relevant to your family, then discuss it in the light of helping others.

63. Deal with adolescent depression

Consider a child's heated feelings seriously. According to the book, *Youth Suicide Depression and Loneliness*, people who commit suicide do not always leave notes. They are not always psychotic or mentally ill. They do not belong to a particular socioeconomic group. They do not talk of suicide to just get attention. You can do something, but you cannot just get them out of the hump automatically, it takes time.[2] Help your child to problem solve, and then try to lighten the situation.

You can identify a depressed child if he uses such phrases as, "Nobody cares, I might as well be dead," and "I never do anything right." He may be negative much of the time, and feel empty, alone, and cut-off. You must take such negative behavior as a warning signal—that is, your child may experience depression, may see no way out of predicaments, and may need someone like yourself with a positive outlook to help him work through this despair.

Assist in the following ways: (a) Identify the problem. "How are you doing?…No, I mean how are you *really* doing? Are you worried about something? Is there anything I should know? How can I help? I'm really concerned." Be calm; give your child time to talk. (b) Listen and empathize as mentioned in Exercise 4. (c) Show you care by using questions about good solutions. (d) Help your child identify one or more of these solutions. (e) Finally, approve a resolution of your agreement. Using steps (a) to (e), what would you say, for instance, if your child said, "I never have friends"?

(a) _____

(b) _____

(c) _____

(d) _____

(e) _____

Positive attitudes bring happiness in families and closeness to God. Faith, "a glad heart," "love," and "the light of the eyes" (Proverbs 15:3,13,15,17,30) are strategies against depression. Now, add another step: (f) Help your child keep a positive attitude. Consider the same situation and add some of the strategies mentioned above (faith, "a glad heart," and so forth), and make it into a composed, positive, learnable, and perhaps even an enjoyable situation.

(f)_____

Because death of a loved one is an especially difficult hurdle to overcome, here is an example of how you could discuss it with a child by using steps (a) to (f):

(a) Identify the problem: Be truthful. Instead of making it appear that death isn't final or that a big bad god snatched this person away, remind them that all of us hope to meet in heaven.

(b) Listen and empathize: When a death occurs, children need to recall the event with someone who listens. They need permission to cry and be angry. Replace the words "Be strong," and "Now you're the man," with "Cry as much as you want," and "I'm sorry this happened. You must feel lonesome."

(c) Ask questions about good solutions: Say, "I care about you. What could we do to make you feel better?"

(d) Identify good solutions: Ask your child to go to the funeral, to say the final good bye, and to reminisce.

(e) Approve a resolution of your agreement: After the funeral is over and the friends have gone, allow children to talk about the death whenever they want. Talk about the good times they had together—the laughter, the hugs, the events, and the friends they shared. Fond memories make life suddenly seem better again. For example, listen to any dinner conversation. Most of the conversation is about things that happened in the past. If we repressed a child from talking about his memories of a loved one, it would be like silencing friends at a dinner party. Much of the time we live in our memories. Learn to express those good times together.

(f) Keep positive attitudes: Help them find new laughter, hugs, moments, events, and friends to share.

What seems a common problem to a parent, can be a monumental one for a child. Children need to know you (and God) care about them. Sister Mary Rose McGready of Covenant House says, "In the turbulence of growing up, it is important for us parents to remember (even if our teens seem to forget) that we love each other. In the end, that's what makes the whole struggle worthwhile."[3]

64. Reduce and manage stress

Teach your children how to adjust to heated situations. John learned about revenge from his favorite television program when the leading character dumped a flowerpot on his ex's living room floor and then threatened to kill himself. Jason, on the other hand, learned from his church and his parents to sit down, work things out, and say the words of confession, "I'm sorry" and "I forgive." Not too many people would have a hard time figuring out which one of the above coped better with life as a young adult.

Contrary to the popular belief that says revenge is sweet, how many vengeful people do you know who are happy and free of stress? There are few, if any, to be certain. Animosities and the lack of forgiveness destroy our well-being and cause us stress. In contrast, working things out through confession, forgiveness, restitution, and thankfulness for God's blessings is the best defense we have against stressful situations.

Stress often precedes depression and suicide. Think about a stressful situation you might have had, and about how good you felt when someone sat down and talked to you and expressed forgiveness, sorrow, and gratitude. Even if the two of you had differences only minutes before, that person's reconciliation most likely gave you an uplifting experience. If so, describe the good feeling.

_____

_____

_____

_____

If these feelings felt good for you, think how the same types of statements can feel good for your children. From the Bible, name various forms of confession, forgiveness, and gratitude (cf. Colossians 3:1-17) you can use in your family. Consider especially the Sacrament of Reconciliation discussed ahead in Exercise 71, and use it as an activity for this or another learning session.

_____

_____

_____

_____

Tell your children that suicide is wrong. Tell them before they experience it first-hand at a funeral of a loved one. Show them why suicide is never a good way to "get even" with those who treat them badly. Teach them how to honor their God-given life, and talk out their problems in a positive way as described in Exercise 63. Teach them that if someone bothers you with angry put-downs and teasing, it reflects badly on the other person, not you. Teach them why suicide isn't a noble way to solve one's problems. Fears dissolve tomorrow, failing grades were yesterday, spoiled friendships disappear, angry feelings cease, embarrassment lasts only a moment, lost tournaments vanish, but suicide lasts an eternity. Teach them how suicide and revenge are sins against the fifth commandment (cf. Exodus 20:13 and Matthew 5:21-22).

Explain in your own words what you need to tell your children about suicide, revenge, problem solving, and faith. Explain how they should thank God because they learned something by their mistakes and embarrassing moments. Last, show them how they can move on to a happy, fulfilled life. Death is never the answer.

_____

_____

_____

_____

Talk to your children about suicide prevention not only for their own benefit, but for the benefit of anyone they may be able to help. On the other hand, if you wait to discuss this matter after a friend commits suicide, it is too late for a couple of reasons: a. It is too late in times of sorrow and extraordinary stress of suicide to let children find out why it is wrong. Homilists at a funeral, after all, have to comfort and assure the afflicted. They may not be giving moral sermons on suicide. b. It is obviously too late to learn how to identify the telltale signs of suicide so that they can try to stop the suicidal loved one who is already dead!

Depressed children may very well be insecure children. They must recognize that they are not alone in experiencing at least a few feelings of insecurity. Insecure feelings manifest into mood changes, reclusion, belligerence, silliness, and smugness. You may need to review together at least some exercises from Chapters I and III. Make a special note to help them develop genuine friendships.

Depressed children need to feel important. They might respond to these ideas:

* Take one day at a time. Recall some pleasurable events, clubs, and hobbies your child liked in the past, and think of how you can help them participate in those same good times again.

* Get enough rest, eat well, and exercise.

* Work together to help those less fortunate. Give your children a chance to find new friends and new experiences. Help your children choose uplifting projects.

* Talk about mistakes, misery, fears, and grievances, but refuse to dwell on these forever. Forgive those who anger you, it does no good to blame others for your misery, even if they are at fault. Resentment only makes you feel worse. Rather, teach children to count their blessings. Worry never helped any situation. Mark Twain said, "I have known many troubles—most of them never happened."

* Congregate as a family for either quiet prayer or songs of praise and gladness.

* Find happiness with other families through involvement in community and Church where faith and goodness abound.

* Occasionally, do something special with each child like stopping for a soda on the way home from the grocery store. Occasionally doing something nice together is not overindulgence that produces self-centered children.

Even if your children are not depressed, choose some of the above. Staying away from the heat is good prevention.

65. Deal with temporary causes of depression

The feelings mentioned in Exercises 63 and 64 (negativity, emptiness, aloneness, revenge, insecurity, moodiness, reclusion, belligerence, silliness, and smugness) may call for professional attention. These could be the signs of suicidal thoughts, and should not be taken lightly. The following are other signs of suicide and depression: giving things away, lacking of friends, complaining of boredom, having decreased energy and sleep disturbances, worrying about weight, losing appetite, experiencing suicide of a close friend or relative, running away, depending on drugs and alcohol, having difficulty concentrating, feeling guilt, crying excessively, changing hygiene patterns, being disturbed then happy, and talking of suicide.

How would you explain to your children the signs of depression and the importance of getting emergency help from parents or professionals?

_____

_____

_____

Tell your children that when they or someone they know has the signs of suicide, one should examine if there is an outside influence hastening the depressed feelings. Are there abuses at home or away, from family or friends? Are drugs, alcohol, or sex involved? Are children having problems with sports, school, or an after school job? If so, discuss it, but perhaps this calls for professional assistance. For a crisis with your family or friends, you may need support from any of these sources—a clergyman, parent support group, teacher, counselor, physician, psychotherapist—immediately.

For further information about depression, check the bibliography at end of chapter.

66. Turn toward God

God does not want us to be depressed. He wants us not only to live a happy life, but he wants us to give happiness to others. He wants us to be close to him now and in all eternity. Happiness in all eternity may be impossible if we choose suicide. Pray as in Psalm 40 [39]:3 "He put a new song in my mouth…" He is with you when you weep. God's love enters your heart and soul through the Holy Spirit. Pray often to him for wisdom.

Create a prayer for the wisdom of the Holy Spirit. Include in it your friends or anyone who seems unhappy and depressed.

_____

_____

_____

Delinquency and Gangs

Preventing gangs and delinquency is like preventing fires. If you were asleep and the kitchen was ablaze, you would need the dependence of an alarm system. So it is with young people, they need the confidence that a good security alert gives them before they confront the fires on their street corners (and unfortunately their homes). Security comes from family, community, church, business, and police that are alert to the flare of crime and to the ways of preventing it.

In the book *People and Folks*, John M. Hagedorn relates this to the prevention of gangs and crime:

> Most adolescents in American society walk a tightrope between conventionality and wildness. Gang members are different only because they are tipped toward wildness—and they need most urgently more weight on the other side and more opportunity to become conventional.[4]

Note that all gang members are not delinquent, and all delinquents are not gang members. Generally, gangs and/or delinquency form because there is a lack of fathers in the home. The next three exercises deal with ways you can make a peaceful society.

67. Role of the Father

Gang members and/or delinquents tend to have dysfunctional families, and the problem promises to get worse for next generation's child. They are born into a world of one-parent families, many of whom are teenagers. *Communiqué* news reports:

> In a series of eight studies performed by the Robin Hood Foundation in New York, findings demonstrated that children born to teens are 50% more likely to repeat a school grade and 170% more likely to go to jail than those children born to mothers in their early twenties.[5]

An enormous divorce rate also adds to the dysfunction of families. Families need dads. Boys especially need a strong male role model to help them grow into responsible men. In reality, families need both moms and dads working together as a loving and caring husband and wife.

Boys, specifically, need to see the strength a dad brings into the family in times of trouble—when the car breaks down, when the kids skip school, when the family needs food, when everyone is sick. His masculinity gives them confidence. His authority gives them hope. His presence gives them security. His faith leads them to God. His good example teaches a son to trust in the Father and to be a good father for the next generation.

Youth sometimes feel a need for protection when they live in urban areas, and sometimes they find it within the realms of a gang. They want to help each other, especially if they are of the same nationality. Gang protection, though, leads to fighting, guns, and stealing. Children deserve security, good schools, good jobs, and skills even if that means moving away from the situation. They need to understand ethnic diversity, and they need parents who understand the first signs of trouble.

The following is a list of things you (especially fathers) can do to improve families and their environment, and to prevent violence in your area:

* Teach love and forgiveness. This seems like a simplistic answer for a mammoth problem, but bear in mind that God moves mountains. Teaching about love and forgiveness brings a sense of security. Secure children have no need for the protection of gangs. Your children, though, may feel anything but loving and forgiving at any given time. Give them a chance to get things off their chests. Use your communication and listening skills, find out what is bothering them, and find out how you can help solve particular problems. (Refer to Exercises 4, and 21 to 24)

* Find out how your children can have either smaller classes or more teachers and volunteers at their schools so that children can feel like individuals and not numbers. Small environments tend to make children feel safe and secure. This helps children learn better, follow discipline better, and have a better sense of belonging.

* Participate in ethnic festivals and study different ethnic cultures with your children so that they can appreciate diverse cultures around them.

* Be aware of gang terminology in your area. If your child starts talking gang lingo, it is time to speak to your child.

* Be aware of gang colors and symbols. If your children and their friends wear similar mysterious items, ask questions.

* Encourage employers to provide full-time employment to heads-of-households so that one parent can feasibly be at home with children. Violent crimes are committed by juveniles more at three P.M. than at any other time of the day, according to the U.S. Department of Justice.[6] Try to be home at this hour. Of course, children need quality time, but they need quantity time, too, if possible. Quality and quantity time keeps children off the streets, keeps them from bonding with the wrong crowds, and helps them converse and bond with adults. Quality and quantity time helps them know you care about them more than you care about money or career, and it helps them understand the art of parenting. Find ideas for parents pressed for time in Exercise 48.

* Help youth from underprivileged backgrounds find full-time employment and rehabilitation by encouraging them to learn new skills, and by lending them your time and money. "…[L]ove your enemies, and do good, and lend, expecting nothing in return…" (Luke 6:35).

* Teach your children saving skills and honest money management.

* Ask your children to avoid anyone who suggests that drugs and drug deals are safe, fun, and profitable.

* According to the book, *Confronting a Culture of Violence,*

> The most violent place in America is not in our streets, but in our homes. Their partner or ex-partner kills more than 50 percent of the women murdered in the United States. Millions of children are victims of family violence.[7]

Show your family how to have fun together and how to venture beyond the four walls. You do not need a costly vacation. Instead, take a trip to the park, a drive to the country, or a walk along a riverbank. Happiness is a choice. Although we must have serious concerns about violence, God's generosity transcends. God spreads the "good news." Go outside and look at the hundreds of things for which to be thankful. Learn to make fun out of dire situations, the rain on a picnic, the snow on Easter. Happiness is an attitude; it makes us look and feel good. It improves our health, our marriages, our families, and our spiritual life. Gratitude and laughter may be the most important things a family shares all day.

* Give your children balance in mental, physical, and spiritual needs:

<u>Mental</u>: Children need conversation with you. Assess if your household is happy or sad. If it is positive, children likely will be open to golden moments of conversation and direction.

Physical: Children need exercise and nutrition. It's more fun and more rewarding for kids if Dad is the Saturday morning coach on their own front yard, than having to always play with strangers at the local gym. Then too, Mom's cooking gives the whole house a warm atmosphere and provides good nutrition.

Spiritual: Children need prayer with the family each day. Include Bible, Catechism, or other spiritual readings. Discuss fear, awe, and respect for the Lord. Read in the *Catechism of the Catholic Church* how children learn to respect their parents: "…This respect has its roots in the fear of God, one of the gifts of the Holy Spirit."[8]

* Create a home atmosphere where your children and their friends are welcome. Your home doesn't need to be expensive; it just needs to be comfortable and clean.

* Explain to your child that fighting is not acceptable. People who make you mad are not worth fighting; fighting only creates more feelings of hostility, especially if you win and they lose, and we won't even survey the other alternative, *your* losing! Teach children to stay away from the near occasion of sin by not preoccupying themselves with an opponent. Teach them that people who put them down are feeling badly about themselves, and fighting cures nothing. Teach them about the honor and strength of walking away. Teach them to avoid delinquents, especially those who feel condemned by you if you refuse to go along with their mischievous schemes. They feel they must pull you into their evil activities to condone their own bad behavior. Teach them it's all right if you don't get along with absolutely everyone. Show them how leaving others alone in difficult situations is a learned practice. Reveal to them how their Christian behavior sometimes speaks louder than words. Show them how to pray for the "bad guy."

* Additional ways you can change a disorganized community:

_____

_____

_____

_____

_____

Circle the ways you can make a difference, and then discuss it with your children.

68. Help for families without fathers (or mothers)

For single mothers, find father figures, (single fathers, find mother figures) in your children's lives through extended family, school, sports, church, youth groups, community volunteers, police activity leagues, and so forth.

* Find friends and family who are willing to take your son fishing or your daughter roller-skating. Let them experience the goodness of "family." Choose people you know and trust. Organizations within your Church can direct you.

* Help children gain a bright outlook for school and for their future at an early age. Ask them thought-provoking questions such as the following: "What do you want to be five or ten years from now?" If a school problem stems from bad experiences with acquaintances, ask: "How can we make it better?"

* Establish supervised entertainment for youth in schools, churches, and homes with a large number of adults present. Work to make existing activities better and more effective in the fight against crime. One ex-delinquent put it this way; "Kids get more recreation in prison than they do in their own neighborhoods." Blow the alert and provide activities such as art, music, and sports to keep children away from the hotbed of dangerous neighborhoods, underprivileged lifestyles, and the allure of the drug money. Show them a better way to live. Reassure your children that these supervised entertainment areas are usually safe havens for them to find friendships.

* Demand adequate police protection, because it keeps youth from needing to protect themselves. This police protection is opposite from police conflict (after it is too late) that tends to create irrational behavior among delinquents and gang members. In addition, the organization Crimestoppers, Incorporated, and other such self-help groups through the Sheriff's Department, allow private individuals to watch neighborhoods. Parents can support these services with their donations and time. Find "Crimestoppers" in the bibliography.

* Organize the parents in your neighborhood and find out their needs. Brainstorm ways to make your neighborhood more desirable and safe. Find compassion and comfort for unsupervised children. Today's unsupervised child may become tomorrow's unsupervised criminal.

* Move to a safer environment, but remember gangs and violence have also invaded small towns and rural areas. It may be better, therefore, to stay in your area, help your children choose their friends wisely, and work within the community to improve conditions.

Certainly, you have to focus on the violence if it is on your street. However, give 95% of the focus to the kindness, honesty, love, sincerity, and hard work of God-loving people. These are the everyday acquaintances that bring us food and shelter, and who do painstaking work to make this a better world. Discuss any ideas above that might make life for you or your neighbors better.

_____

_____

_____

69. Gangs and SCARE

Society tells us to beat the system, do what feels good, watch what we want to watch, win at any cost, and refuse to live by our conscience. Explain to your children about the SCARE tactics, from Exercise 25, of gangs and delinquents. Briefly (so as not to frighten) tell them about the secrets and lies of a violent individual, the control of the gang leader, the addiction of the corrupt, the ridicule of the hypocrite, and the excuses of an enemy. Explain that gangs and delinquents may act as though they represent 100% of the population, even if they only comprise a small part of it. Use the SCARE acronym to keep your children from corruption and gangs:

Secrets: Remind your children that it is no secret, a thief didn't go from being a saint to being a thief overnight. We become bad in little increments. Communicate the truth about what is right and wrong, teach about honesty, and expect good behavior in your children from an early age. Make sure they understand that crime is not an acceptable practice, even if these are small crimes such as cheating at football, stealing paper clips, jaywalking, and hitting a classmate. Teach them there is honor in doing what is right and pleasing to God. "For Christ is the end of the law, that every one who has faith may be justified" (Romans 10:4).

Control: Gang leaders try to control your children. Counter this by discussing inspiring news articles or your own family's heroic stories with your children. Tell how people of good character do good deeds for others; they do not manipulate us.

Addiction: Realize that children can become addicted to corruption on television, videos, video games, and movies whether they are alone or with others. You have the right and responsibility to monitor these pastimes. For movie ratings by the U.S. Catholic Conference Office, see the bibliography. Many children are just plain lonely and they hide behind loud music, television sets, or questionable

154 • Speak to Your Children

friends. They don't know how to relate to people. Review Exercise 26 for information on developing friendships to help children if they are lonely.

Ridicule: Refuse to let your children be ridiculed by their friends. These so-called "friends" portray evil as good and good as evil. Help your children distinguish the difference. Explain that one cannot love God, and then show you how to sniff helium. When you refuse, they ridicule you. They are bad news.

Excuses and Enemies: Refuse to support the enemy, for instance the undesirable media, and let them know about it. Keep local radio and television telephone numbers posted and call them. Be calm and reasonable as you let them know about your objections. Ask them to replace certain programs. Be specific. (Use "I want," "I expect," "I need," "I like," and "fact" statements followed with reasonable expectations.) Think twice, however, before you blame the media for all our ills. The media only reflects our moral (or immoral) lives. Closer to the problem lies our excuses, because often we lack religious beliefs and responsible government policies.

Though your government may be one of the best, it is wrong if officials support the death penalty (when non-destructive restraints are available), distribute intravenous needles for illegal drugs, give contraceptives to teens, or approve abortion. The public, then, begins to believe in it. Therefore, elect upstanding moral leaders in the government. Consider running for an office yourself. Pray with your children, that Christianity makes a bigger impact on government, the media, and our lives.

How would you explain the words of St. Thomas Aquinas, who said, "Impurity leads inevitably to violence"?

_____

_____

_____

_____

One excellent thing you can do is to teach your children to be pillars in the community. Enter children into leadership programs such as "4-H Clubs of America" sponsored by the County Cooperative Extension office. Volunteers teach children various basic skills such as cooking, sewing, and caring for pets and other animals. The 4-H pledge is, "I pledge my head to clearer thinking, my heart to greater loyalty, my hands to larger service, and my health to better living, for my club, my community, my country, and my world."

Bishop Sheen said, "Violence is due to want of faith, but there is no evidence that faith cannot cure."[9] Mountains of faith and good works bring children off the streets.

Note: *The Catechism of the Catholic Church* said, "The power of Satan is, nonetheless, not infinite. He is only a creature...."[10] We can overcome evil. We will not wait until our children fall into the pit of depression, and the web of delinquency and gang activity. Instead, we will prevent atrocities by communicating the facts to our children and by creating a better home, church, and community involvement for them with the emphasis always on goodness and faith. "We know that...God works for good with those who love him..." (Romans 8:28). Forward now to ways of "Defending the Faith," the final building blocks that seal and mold a child's conscience.

Endnotes:

1. *Catechism of the Catholic Church* (Washington, D.C.: United States Catholic Conference, 1997), Publication no. 5-110, #2280, p. 550.

2. Brent Q. Hafen and Kathryn J. Frandsen, *Youth Suicide: Depression and Loneliness* (Evergreen, CO: Cordillera Press, Inc., 1986), pp. 18-25.

3. Sister Mary Rose McGready, *Are You out there, God?* (New York: Covenant House, 1996), p. 111.

4. John M. Hagedorn, *People and Folks* (Chicago: Lake View Press, P.O. Box 578279, Chicago, Illinois 60657, 1988), p. 17.

5. Jody Oaks at Campaign for Our Children 1-410-576-9000, as cited in "Pregnancy Costs Studied," *Communiqué* news (26 July 1996): p. 1-2.

6. FBI, 1993, national incident-based reporting system 1991-1992, cited in *Combating Violence and Delinquency: The National Juvenile Justice Action Plan Report* (Washington DC: U.S. Department of Justice office of Juvenile Justice and Delinquency Prevention, March 1996), p. 52.

7. "Violence Against Women," *Journal of the American Medical Association*, June 17, 1992, as cited in *Confronting a Culture of Violence*, a Pastoral Message of the U.S. Catholic Bishops, Office for Publishing and Promotion Services, Publication No. 028-1 (Washington, DC: United States Catholic Conference, n.d.), p. 4.

8. *Catechism of the Catholic Church*, op. cit., #2217, p. 535.

9. Bishop Fulton J. Sheen, *Walk With God* (New York: Maco Magazine Corporation, 1965), p. 53.

10. *Catechism of the Catholic Church*, op. cit., #395, p. 99.

Bibliography:

American Psychiatric Association. *Let's Talk Facts About Depression*. Washington, DC 20005: Public Affairs, Department P, 1400 K Street, N.W.

Amstutz, Wendell. *Youth Violence*, the belief behavior connection. Rochester, MN, 55903: National Community Resource Center, P.O. Box 89, 1998.

Combating Violence and Delinquency: The National Juvenile Justice Action Plan Report. Washington, D.C. 20531: U.S. Department of Justice, Office of Justice Programs, Office of Juvenile Justice and Delinquency Prevention.

Covenant House, getting in touch with people who can help you in your hometown. Telephone: 1-800-999-9999.

Crimestoppers Inc., self-help group that allows private individuals to watch on neighborhoods. Albuquerque, NM 87110: Room, 104, 8100 Mountain Road, N E.

D/ART/Public Inquiries, on depression. Rockville, MD 20857: National Institute of Mental Health, Room 15C-05, 5600 Fishers Lane.

Girls and Boystown Hotline, for children in crisis. Telephone: 1-800-448-3000.

Hafen, Brent Q. and Kathryn J. Frandsen. *Youth Suicide Depression and Loneliness.* Evergreen, CO: Cordillera Press, Inc., 1986.

McGready, Sister Mary Rose. *Are You out there God?* New York: Covenant House, 1996.

U.S. Catholic Conference, office of film and broadcasting, for movie ratings, Telephone: 1-800-311-4"ccc".

U.S. Catholic Conference of Catholic Bishops. *Confronting a Culture of Violence,* publication No. 028-1. Washington, D.C.: United States Catholic Conference, Inc., Telephone: 1-800-235-USCC, Web site: http://www.nccbuscc.org, outside of United States call 1-301-209-9020, 1994.

Violence Resource Guide, twenty-page prevention guide, publication WX-222. South Burlington, Vermont 05407: WNET, Education Broadcasting, Telephone: 1-800-336-1917.

Wood, Steve with James Burnham. *Christian Fatherhood,* cassettes. Port Charlotte, FL 33949: Family Life Center Publications, P.O. Box 6060, Telephone: 1-941-764-8565, Web site: www.dads.org, 1998.

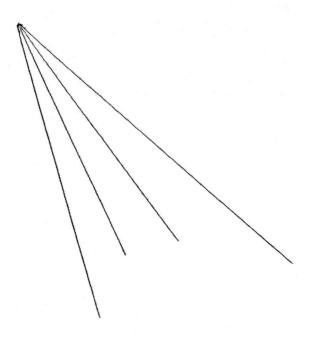

How can we be certain our children live according to
what we discussed? The answer lies in Christian truth.

Chapter VII

Defend the Faith

"But they who wait for the Lord shall renew their strength, they shall mount up with wings like eagles, they shall run and not be weary, they shall walk and not faint" (Isaiah 40:31).

You may ask: "Then, what more can we give our children? We shared the foundation of self-worth through God's love in Chapter I, discipline in Chapter II, and resistance to negative influences in Chapter III. We applied it in Chapters IV, V and VI, but how can we be certain our children live according to what we discussed?" The answer lies in Christian truth. This is the final building block to good behavior. Our children's morals do not crumble if they have faith in God (cf. Hebrews 12:10-16).

In teaching faith principles, children need role models, and they need explanations about the Church. They need a chance to put faith into action. They also need to understand how other belief systems differ from Catholicism, and how some are downright dangerous.

This is what the *Catechism of the Catholic Church* says about hope for our families:

> Parents' respect and affection are expressed by the care and attention they devote to bringing up their young children and *providing for their physical and spiritual needs*. As the children grow up, the same respect and devotion lead parents to educate them in the right use of their reason and freedom.[1]

Continue now to the roof, the cap, the lid that guides, protects, and fosters your child's morality.

(Again, as you speak with your children, follow instructions from the Introduction on the suitable age for each child.)

Answer Children's Questions about the Faith

Ending this book without a few words on the Christian faith would be like ending the "Our Father" without an "Amen." Your children learn bits and pieces, here and there, about their faith. However, until you teach the final "Amen" on their basic beliefs, they may not continue with the faith as you hoped.

What would happen if a child had a paper route and didn't know the basics of being a good carrier? He did not deliver papers on a regular basis. He never read his instructions. He did not communicate with the publishers. He knew little about the newspaper, and he seldom contacted his subscribers. Soon, his job would cease to exist. Yet, all too often, children know the basics of their religion with the same indifference as our example of the paper carrier. By the time they graduate from high school, their faith vanishes. Their faith had little chance of carrying into their adult world.

Instead, parents can learn to be the primary teachers of faith to children. The basics of keeping them interested in the faith involve attending weekly church services, having the means available to study the truth, communicating your faith with children, helping them develop a discerning conscience, and showing them how to put their faith to work.

If you affirm for instance, what your children already learned in Christian education classes, they become carriers of the faith. This support helps them choose good decisions in life, enjoy peace, and carry on their Catholic faith for future generations. They will have the last Amen. Psalm 95:1 says you should "make a joyful noise…" You will find many discussion ideas for any child, but mostly for the 12 to 14-year-old.

70. Understand the third commandment

The third commandment states, "'Remember the [S]abbath day, to keep it holy'" (Exodus 20: 8). The more ways we teach our children at the youngest ages to lovingly adhere to this, the more faithful they will be to the Church. Circle and discuss some ways you might improve your family's observance of this Commandment.

* Attend Mass faithfully on Sundays and holy days and be thankful for it. Send the message to your children that worshipping God at Mass is the most impor-

tant event in your week. It is at the top of your list. On the other hand, to skip Mass tells kids that loving him, honoring him, and serving him is not as important as whatever else kept you at home. "For a day in thy courts is better than a thousand elsewhere…" (Psalm 84:10).

* Make church attendance a delightful thing to do and a place they "get to" go, instead of a place they "have to" go. Relate humorous stories from your background that happened in church. One teen choir member from a small Midwestern town relates this witticism: "One Holy Thursday afternoon, our 'fresh-from-New-York-City-priest' needed a bucket for the holy water. However, unbeknownst to him, he purchased instead a porcelain enamel potty from his small town hardware store. That evening, my fellow singers and I viewed him from our lookout high in the choir loft. We chortled as Father strutted down the isle, potty in hand, sprinkling everyone with his 'blest water'."

* Show the serious side of Mass, too. Imagine that Jesus came to your door and invited your family to his Last Supper on Earth. You knew the people in town were upset because Jesus destroyed their superstitious beliefs, and they were so mad they wanted him tried in criminal court. First, you repent directly to Jesus (in confession) because you may have hurt him, too. Then you say you will come to his meal, immediately. You quickly find proper clothing, and arrive as soon as possible. You silently empathize with Jesus and again tell him you are sorry for all his hurts. You sit in glory, praise, and thanksgiving for the sacrifice he gives you.

* Let your children know it is a serious matter if they don't attend Mass on Sundays and other holy days of obligation. In the United States, the other holy days of obligation are: Christmas (Dec. 25), Solemnity of the Mother of God (Jan. 1), Ascension Thursday, the Assumption (Aug. 15), All Saints' Day (Nov. 1), and the Immaculate Conception (Dec. 8).

* Be faithful in other church functions aside from Sunday and holy days, especially during Advent and Lent.

* Attend adult faith sharing groups while your children attend their Christian education classes.

* Make Sundays and holy days into family days in which you renew the soul and body, and not into days where everyone catches up on all the work.

* Attend Sunday and holy day Masses when traveling so that your children understand their obligation to this important matter. (Refer ahead to Exercise 71 on the precepts of the Church.) This also helps children become accustomed to participating in services away from home when they reach adulthood and no longer live with you.

* Talk about your faith and love for Jesus not only on Sundays, but all week long. Let your children understand how prayer, faith, and good works are a part of our very being. The Bible says, "build yourselves up on your most holy faith; pray in the Holy Spirit;" (Jude 20). Let your children know that love works both ways: Jesus loves them, too.

* Make some friendships with other Catholic families. Friendships within the Church help children become more closely united with the Faith.

* Support clergy and others working in the Church. They are human and need understanding and encouragement. Jesus, too, was human and disturbed many of his would-be followers. Too often, we mistakenly rate the best priest by modern standards of entertainment. For example, they have to be positive thinkers, make a good appearance, have an impeccable personality, and have the most permissive ideas. However, Christ, our first priest, never came to this earth to entertain and to tell us only what we wanted to hear. He upset a few people. He chased the moneychangers from the temple, he had enemies such as Judas and Pontius Pilate, and he ate with the prostitutes and tax collectors. The firmest priests, like Jesus, may teach you the most. Help your children accept the clergy for who they are.

* Refuse to be mastered by a spirit of hopelessness. Turn instead toward the blessings of God's love. If you don't feel comfortable about teaching your children the faith, take a course from your local parish priest, or read *Catechism of the Catholic Church*, and find books, tapes, or magazines by Benkovic, Budnik, Currie, Fox, Hahn, Keating, Madrid, Ray, Staples, Stravinskas, Suprenant, and others listed in the bibliography. If your children go to college, have them inquire about the Fellowship of Catholic University Students "FOCUS" group that has a strong foundation of student leaders. They conduct Bible studies on campus. This, too, is in the bibliography.

* Contribute time, talent, and money to the Church and compliment your children if they also participate.

* Pray for (and with) your children so that they keep the faith. Begin with a fervent Sign of the Cross.

* Other_____

The seven gifts of the Holy Spirit are wisdom, understanding, counsel, fortitude, knowledge, piety, and fear of the Lord. What better place could we receive these riches than through the Catholic Church? Discuss the above with your children.

71. Understand the Church

Jesus founded one Church, and he promised it would never be destroyed. As your children mature, they learn about the Church in Christian education classes. You, too, can supplement your insight about the virtues of the Church. Listed below are a few:

* **Authority of the Pope:** Jesus said to Peter, "And I tell you, you are Peter, and on this rock I will build my church, and the powers of death shall not prevail against it" (Matthew 16:18). Does this mean we will never have Catholics who sin? No, Judas sinned against Jesus. He was a primary cause of the crucifixion, and he was one of the first Apostles. Matthew 16:18 means that the (Catholic) Church will prevail until the end of time, in spite of all who sin.

* **Mass:** The Mass is the perpetuation of the Sacrifice of the Cross. We gather to adore, praise, and thank God.

* **Prayers:** Apostles' Creed, Our Father, Hail Mary, and so forth. Find prayers at back of book.

* **Sacraments:** The sacraments are supernatural outward signs, instituted by Jesus Christ to give grace. The ordained priest acts in the person of Christ when each sacrament is administered. The seven sacraments follow:

a. **Baptism:** In this sacrament, we are cleansed of all original and personal sin, and we become reborn in Jesus Christ. He said, "...I say to you, unless one is born of water and the spirit, he cannot enter the kingdom of God." (John 3:5). The priest usually administers this sacrament to children at two or three weeks of age. When there is serious reason, anyone with the right intentions to baptize, as the Catholic Church prescribes, may do so by pouring water over the forehead while saying: "I baptize you in the name of the Father and of the Son and of the Holy Spirit." This sacrament opens the door to other sacraments.

b. **Reconciliation:** Scripture says, "All this is from God, who through Christ reconciled us to himself and gave us the ministry of reconciliation," (2 Corinthians 5:18). Before Reconciliation, first, we examine our conscience. Then, in private confession (another form with general confession and general absolution is for only grave situations), we tell our mortal sins. A mortal sin is committed if one has full knowledge and complete consent of the will. This is a grievous sin against the will of God, such as knowing and willfully breaking the Ten Commandments or the precepts (ahead in this exercise) of the Church. Second, we have sorrow for all sins, even venial sins, which are lesser everyday faults. Third, we promise to avoid near occasions of sin. Fourth, we confess every grave sin since our last confession. Confessing venial sin, however, is not necessary but highly commended. This is how the confession starts: The priest begins with a Sign of the Cross and a greeting. Then, we can say something like the following: Bless me, Father, I have sinned. My last confession was_____(once a month is about right for most Catholics or whenever we have a mortal sin). I loved God in this special way_____, but I have sometimes failed, too. I am sorry for the sins I committed _____. Fifth, we do penance the priest gives, and try to repair any harm. Note: We must be free of sin (especially mortal sin through the sacrament of Penance) before receiving other sacraments, except for Baptism that removes sin. If we realized the benefits of Penance, we would eagerly do this before Saturday's ballgame!

c.   **Eucharist:** In the Eucharist, the bread and wine become the body and blood of Christ. This is called transubstantiation and is done by a validly ordained priest at the consecration of the Mass. Jesus said, "'…I say to you, unless you eat the flesh of the Son of man and drink his blood, you have no life in you'" (John 6: 53). Learning about the Eucharist may be easier if you understand it through some recent converts to Catholicism. Their son was about to receive his First Holy Communion. Kimberly Hahn related the following when asked by her husband, Scott, "Can you imagine what the angels must think?":

> Certainly the angels are present for the liturgy…. They must peer down in wonder and awe at the incredible love our heavenly Father had for us in sending Jesus to earth to take on lowly human nature, to lay down that life in sacrifice for us and, finally, to feed us with that resurrected and glorified offering of his Body and Blood. What a glorious mystery!

She further states:

> Fasting for the hour beforehand has been a good experience, too, because it has been a small mortification (of which there are all too few in my life) to point to my need to hunger for souls.[2]

In the Sacrifice of the Mass, Jesus offers us the Eucharist without the bloodshed of the cross.

d. **Confirmation:** Jesus proclaimed us as witnesses to the faith. Acts 2:3 speaks of "tongues as of fire…" from the Holy Spirit. Confirmation arms us to be mature Christians entirely akin to Christ, enlists us in his service forever, protects us in tribulation, and makes us soldiers for the Church.

e. **Holy Orders:** Deacons, priests, and bishops become ordained to minister to the people (cf. Romans 10:14,15,17 and 15:15-16). Bishops ordain priests with the sacred power and grace to sanctify others through the Holy Spirit.

f. **Marriage:** Husband and wife are united forever in the exclusive union and sacred contract, matrimony. "Be subject to one another out of reverence for Christ" (Ephesians 5:21). "[A] man shall leave his father and mother…" (Ephesians 5:31).

g. **Anointing of the Sick:** It is also known as a "sacrament of the dying." The priest prays for the restoration of body and soul, and anoints with the oil of the sick (cf. James 5:14-15).

* **Bible:** The Bible includes twenty-seven books of the New Testament. The Catholic, Eastern Orthodox, and Anglican Bibles include forty-six books of the Old Testament, whereas some Protestant Bibles include thirty-nine books. Note: Catholics, with the inspiration of the Holy Spirit from the time of Christ, wrote the Bible. It says the Bible does not contain all of divine revelation (cf. John 21:25 and 2 Thessalonians 2:15). Some divine revelation is also found in Sacred Tradition (cf. 2 Timothy 2:1-2) and handed down by the Catholic Church.

* **Precepts of the Catholic Church:** The precepts were decreed by pastoral authorities and described in the *Catechism of the Catholic Church* as our minimal duty:

First, "You shall attend Mass on Sundays and on holy days of obligation and rest from servile labor."
Second, "You shall confess your sins at least once a year."
Third, "You shall receive the sacrament of the Eucharist at least during the Easter season."
Fourth, "You shall observe the days of fasting and abstinence established by the Church."
Fifth, "You shall help to provide for the needs of the Church."[3]

The *Catechism of the Catholic Church* calls the precepts our minimal obligation:

The precepts of the Church are set in the context of a moral life bound to and nourished by liturgical life. The obligatory character of these positive laws decreed by the pastoral authorities is meant to guarantee to the faithful the very necessary minimum in the spirit of prayer and moral effort, in the growth in love of God and neighbor...[4]

Only grave illness, a serious deed of charity, or moral impossibility excuses us from the precepts. To do less would be a mortal sin. It is as if you were training for the Olympics and you were able-bodied, but did not do the minimum requirement, you would be at risk of not qualifying. Likewise, the Church says that if you do less than the precepts, it would endanger your soul from the great reward of heaven. As in the Olympics, we would strive to do more, not less than the minimum requirements!

* **Complete Christianity**: Refer to 1 Timothy 3:15. Also, the book, *Pillar of Fire Pillar of Truth* said:

> ...Christians [who have split away from the Catholic Church] eliminated some authentic beliefs and added new ones of their own making. The forms of Christianity they established are really incomplete Christianity. Only the Catholic Church was founded by Jesus, and only it has been able to preserve all Christian truth without error—and great numbers of people are coming to see this.[5]

We must welcome our brothers and sisters with warm hearts and open arms.

* **Other terms of faith (among many)**: You may want to review these with your children: angels, Bishop, Christian, grace, God, heaven, hell, hope, Incarnation, indulgences, love, Mary, salvation, sin, Trinity, and so forth. (These are listed in *Catechism of the Catholic Church* referred to in the bibliography.)

How many of these Catholic truths do your children understand?_____ Circle the ones you want to discuss with them. Especially encourage children to practice Reconciliation and the Eucharist often.

Parents assume their children picked up most of these truths from Christian education classes, but do we really know if they grasped the full meaning? Perhaps they were absent when something important was taught, maybe they used a different series of books in later years, or possibly, you switched parishes. It's good to check what they know and don't know. Tell your children you never want them to give up on their beliefs in the Catholic Church.

72. Use parables

One way to gain your children's awareness of Church teaching is to use your own imaginative stories as Jesus did with parables (cf. Matthew 13:1-58). Use a story or incident your children can easily relate to in their particular developmental stage, for instance:

* If your child asks, "Why do we have to go to church?" You could answer, "Going to church is like going to school. Why do you have to go to school?" Listen to what your child says and then answer something like this:… "Going to school is the law of the land. We are privileged to attend, and we have deep need to be educated. Similarly, attendance at church is the law of God. We are privileged to be a member, and we have profound need to learn about a better life through his teachings."

How would you explain the question to your child?

_____

_____

_____

_____

* Your child may ask, "Why do we have a Pope?" You could answer, "Having a Pope for the Church is like having a president for the United States. Why does the United States have a president?…We have a president because he unifies the United States. We have a Pope because he unifies the Church. Can you imagine what the states would be like if we had no president to lead us? Every state would be doing something different. The same would happen if the Church had no Pope."

How would you explain the question to your child?

_____

_____

_____

_____

* Your child may ask, "Why can't a couple just live together? Why should they get married?" You could answer, "A couple needs the marriage covenant like a contractor needs a building permit. Why does one need a permit to build a house?…You need a permit because you want each person's rights protected. The same principle applies to marriage. Mom's, Dad's, and the children's rights are

protected and secure until death if a man and women have a marriage promise to God."

How would you explain the question to your child?

_____

_____

_____

_____

* Your child may ask, "Why can't Catholics divorce?" You could answer by telling them what Jesus said, "Every one who divorces his wife and marries another commits adultery, and he who marries a woman divorced from her husband commits adultery." (Luke 16:18). You could also say, "Jesus knows what is best for us. Going against God's will would be similar to a basketball player in the top number one game of the season who told his coach he wouldn't play the game by the rules—the rules that everyone else had to follow. Why do we have to use the coach's rules?…We abide because he knows what is best. The same principle applies to Jesus' rules. He knows what is best. Marriage partners vow to practice fidelity, indissolubility, openness to children, and mutual self-giving just as the star basketball player vows to follow basketball rules. It's only in rare cases when a basketball coach has to make an exception to a rule, just as there are rare instances when the Church declares a marriage null."

How would you explain the question to your child?

_____

_____

_____

_____

* Your child may ask, "Why do we celebrate holy days?" You could answer, "The Church needs holy days like our country needs holidays. Why do we celebrate Memorial Day?…Because this day is special and we want to show our gratitude for the distinguished occasion. Likewise, we celebrate holy days because they mark special occasions and mysteries of our Faith, and we give God thanks and praise for these blessings."

How would you explain the question to your child?

_____

_____

_____

_____

* Your child may ask, "Why do we worship the Virgin Mary?" You could answer, "We don't worship the Virgin Mary, we honor the Virgin Mary. We honor her on special occasions like we honor a family member on special occasions. Why do we honor your father on Father's Day?...We honor him because he is a great dad, and we want to tell him how much we appreciate him. The same principle applies when we honor the Virgin Mary. She is special, and we want to tell her how much we respect her."

How would you explain the question to your child?

_____

_____

_____

_____

* Your child may ask, "My friends say I'm not saved. Am I saved?" You could answer, "Of course you are saved; not only once, but many times. Being saved once would be like being saved from a serious car accident. Would you only want to be saved once?...Of course not, you might be saved later from pneumonia and need antibiotics. The same idea applies when we are saved through grace. He wants us to preserve our faith and be saved often through sacraments, good works, and more."

How would you explain the question to your child?

_____

_____

_____

_____

Find out how the rich man wanted to save his five brothers (cf. Luke 16:19-31).

* Your child may ask, "Why do we need the Sacrament of Reconciliation?" You could answer, "Let us compare celebrating Reconciliation to someone who has almost drowned and has come back to life. Why would everyone rejoice?...They would celebrate his life because they loved him and wanted him to survive the drowning and live a full life with family and friends. The same is true when we ask forgiveness in Reconciliation. We survive from sin and live a full life united with the goodness of Christ. Now, that's a reason to be overjoyed. Then, by receiving our precious Lord in the Eucharist, we celebrate again."

How would you explain the question to your child?

_____

_____

_____

_____

* If your child asks, "Why does the Church oppose suicide?" You could answer, 'The Church's opposition to this hate crime is similar to a teacher's opposition to fighting, kicking, and slapping in the classroom. Why does a teacher oppose that?…A teacher opposes fighting, kicking, and slapping because it upsets the regular day's routine and hurts all students physically and emotionally. The teacher has to find help for this student so that he can live a quality life. School life is much more pleasant without hateful assault on each other. So too, our Lord stressed how our life in heaven and on earth can become pleasant for us and for everyone involved. We are to try our hardest and to work things out, instead of choosing the vengeance of suicide. Mental health clinics and medical doctors help you overcome depression and relieve pain. The Christian answer to solving affliction is not suicide, regardless of what the euthanasia proponents voice. Our Lord's fifth commandment says, "'You shall not kill….'" (Exodus 20:13). We must obey God's word if we want to be with him eternally. We must promptly find help when we feel bad enough to harm ourselves. (Review Exercises 63-66 for more help on depression and suicide, and Exercise 61, Richard Doerflinger's statement on the "need to respect all human life" even our own.)'

How would you explain the question to your child?

_____

_____

_____

_____

* If your child asks, "Why do we have days of fast and abstinence?" You could answer by saying, 'Why do your parents want you to refrain from cookies before mealtime?…You give up cookies so that you hunger for the main meal. It's the same with fasting and abstinence. We give up food so that we more easily resist evil temptations and therefore feast on God's goodness. Fasting means one full meal and two lighter meals (the two combined should not exceed the full meal) on Ash Wednesday and Good Friday after age 18. Abstinence means no meat on Ash Wednesday and Fridays of Lent after age 14. Every Friday of the year, Catholics have an obligation to offer up some sacrifice (meat, prayer, penance, reconciliation, pilgrimage, fasting, charity, or something else), as Fridays are days

of penance. The Bible asks, "that you abstain from what has been sacrificed to idols and from blood and from what is strangled…" (Acts 15:29).'

How would you explain the question to your children?

_____

_____

_____

* If your child asks, "Why do we have only men priests?" You could say, 'Why did the world need Blessed Teresa of Calcutta?…Jesus knew we needed a good role model for the poor and destitute. Sometimes the world situation gets so desperate that we blindly need what God sends us. He sent us Simon Peter and said, '"I will give you the keys of the kingdom of heaven…"'(Matthew 16: 19). We probably won't fully understand why Simon and the other Apostles were men—Jesus didn't discriminate against women, he chose the crown of thorns and gave Mary the crown of heaven. A step forward in history, though, might give us a clue as to why we need priests as good male role models. Steve Wood, leader of a Catholic men's group called Covenant Keepers, spoke about the decline of men in the family. He said, if men continue to drop out at the present pace, there soon will be no men left in the family.[6] The male population in state and federal prisons is 1,343,164 while the female population is only 97,491.[7] Our Lord knew we needed top-notch male role models, so that the Church and, indeed, all civilization could survive into the twenty-first and twenty-second centuries. Can it be that instead of reproving our male priests, we need to thank them, encourage them, and pray for them—big time? Could it be that God gave women the gift of producing life and made them the image of the Church, and he wanted to give men something great, too, by letting them officiate at the Eucharist? Could it be that we would have more priests if we became more pro-life? Statistics indicate this as true.'

How would you explain the question to your children?

_____

_____

_____

* If your child should ask, "Why do I have to be a Catholic all my life?" You could say, "Staying Catholic is like staying with the safest airplane. Why would you want a safe airplane?…You want a secure aircraft so that it propels you safely to your destination. Choosing one, for example, that was not in top condition

would be dangerous. Similarly, choosing a religion without all the truths it needs to reach an eternity with God in heaven could be disastrous."

How would you explain the question to your children?

_____

_____
_____
_____

Your children may need more information on the following subjects:

* **Purgatory:** Scripture speaks of a cleansing "fire" that wipes away our sins (1 Corinthians 3:15). *Catechism of the Catholic Church,* also speaks of purgatory.[8] Compare it to God's burning love for us.

* **"Whore of Babylon":** This title refers in the Book of Revelation to the pagan city of Rome, not to the Church as some have wrongly accused it. The Romans killed the early Christian martyrs. Compare "Whore of Babylon" to crime in the inner cities and its infringement on the innocent.

* **Authority in the Church:** God gave supernatural revelation to the Church. The Church's teaching authority is called the Magisterium (bishops in union with the Holy Father). David Currie said in his book, *Born Fundamentalist*:

> A careful study of the first recorded church council—even the NIV [New International Version] Bible refers, in Acts 15:1-21, to the "Council of Jerusalem"—led me to interesting conclusions [about the need for authority]...[9]

You might compare the Church's need for authority to a school's need for a school board and its president that helps the system run smoothly.

* **Dogma:** The Church does not invent dogma. Dogma is a clarification of what we already believe. Compare dogma to the Supreme Court decisions on the Constitution of the United States. The Supreme Court defines what the Constitution originally meant to say, just as the Church produces dogma about what we already believe.

* **Justification by faith and good works:** The Bible says not only that salvation comes through faith (cf. Ephesians 2:8), but it also says, "You see that a man is justified by works and not by faith alone" (James 2:24). Compare faith to getting a new computer, and putting forth much effort to make it work for you.

* **Sin and scandal in the Church:** Explain to your child that all denominations of people are sinners, but we must "...Resist the devil..." (James 4:7). Compare it to scandal in the House of Representatives. We would not abandon the House because a few did something wrong. Neither should we abandon the Church because those in its history sinned. Father Robert J. Fox, author of *The Catholic Faith*, gives a brief warning:

> ...[W]hereas the Church founded by Jesus Christ does, indeed, have divine attributes of authority, infallibility and indefectibility and the marks of oneness, holiness, universality and apostolicity, yet, it must still struggle against the forces of evil which have always attempted to destroy it by every means. The divine promise for the universal Church remains, however....[10]

Admitting past sins of people in the Church is good. We must correct them, repent, and make restitution, but we must be careful not to dwell on them centuries later. It would be as if a friend told others of your every sin. God is more concerned about unforgiving "friends" than he is about one who repented and was saved.

* **Inquisitions:** The Church appointed a number of European courts and tribunals, called Inquisitions, beginning in the 13th century to find and suppress heresy. The Holy See protested against excesses, but failed to curb some abuses throughout hundreds of years. Though, according to Karl Keating, Catholic apologist, many untruths about heresies are connected with these Inquisitions. There were "a few thousand," not "millions," convicted as heretics as some incorrect sources said. Torture "was used in nearly <u>all</u> secular courts of the time—it was used in a few cases during the Inquisition." Catholic courts were fair compared to regular courts. To give you an example of standards of those times, the "Protestants in England were burning people by the hundreds on charges of witchcraft, the Spanish Inquisition said that it could find no evidence of witchcraft being practiced—despite numerous baseless accusations!"[11] You might compare the Inquisitions to a fish story: It gets bigger every time it is retold.

Nothing above may seem relevant now, but it is important that children know. As they grow older and various religious groups come knocking on their consciences, they may remember the comparisons you made. Christ wants us to love those who disagree with us. The best way to love them is to pray for them, study about the word of God, and spread the good news to them. How would you tell your children to defend their faith?

_____

_____

_____

_____

List other questions your children might have about the Church and give imaginative ways to answer.

_____

_____

_____

_____

Parables make faith come alive and children love them.

73. Convey truth and depict conflict with SCARE

The second Vatican Council taught, "For the Catholic Church is by the will of Christ the teacher of truth..." (*Declaration on Religious Liberty*, No. 14). Different Catholic sources that convey truth include:

* **Commandments** (Isaiah 48:17-19 and Exodus 20:1-17)

* **Bible** "All scripture is inspired by God and profitable for teaching, for reproof, for correction, and for training in righteousness" (2 Timothy 3:16)

* **Catholic newspapers, magazines, videos, cassettes, and books**—especially on saints' and martyrs' lives and the book *Catechism of the Catholic Church*

* **Clergy and religious** (invite them to your house for a visit, supper, and so forth)

* **Religious symbols** (cross, manger, pictures, and so forth)

* Other _____

Relate how you found value in any above sources.

_____

_____

_____

_____

Circle two or three sources of truth, listed above, that you could bring or invite into your home.

It once was fact, if you picked up a Catholic publication, you were certain to find truth. Presently, though, some "Catholic" readings are questionable. Scan them when they come into your house and cancel the ones that present an opposing view of Church teachings. Some may publish that their group is "more Catholic" than Catholic. Others want to change the Church and make it "progressive" and "enlightened." They omit important doctrine, especially on conscience formation and pro-life. They forget to mention sins such as, sodomy, contraception, and abortion, while they give you their own formula for morality, not God's. They preach rationalism and relativism and call the Church backward or give it a distorted view. They call it judgmental when you respond; yet, they are judgmental, especially against the Church. Be diligent and you will find plenty of inspiring Catholic literature from which to choose. Use the SCARE acronym of Exercise 25, and determine the difference between good Catholic publications and other printings in conflict. Discuss this with your children:

<u>Secrecy</u> _____

<u>Control</u> _____

<u>Addiction</u> _____

<u>Ridicule</u> _____

<u>Excuses/Enemies</u> _____

Attending Catholic meetings at parishes and schools is important. If you go to a "Catholic" meeting and the discussion is contrary to Catholic faith, let them know how you feel and offer another solution. Stand up for what you know is true. New Age and various other dissenting groups have their own morality. Learn to detect hidden messages that confuse or weaken our faith.

You will review the New Age, ahead, in Exercise 78. Other groups may work like this: They wrongly say the papacy is only symbolic or the Church has an authority problem. They imply that since the word moral is derived from the word custom, they can deduce that Christian morality varies for different cultures, which is false. This may open their door to misunderstanding promiscuity, contraception, homosexual lifestyle (sodomy), pedophilia, divorce, abortion, and more. They wrongly state that Church doctrine changes as the Church obtains modern evidence. They speak more of enlightenment than of faith, more of self-absorption than of prayer, more of universal harmony than of good works, more of being divine than of worshiping a divine God. Some claim the Church didn't begin with Jesus, and they spend most of their time enraged about the Church of the Middle Ages. It is evident that sin was not relegated to the Middle Ages!

Many good-willed people may not know Catholic truth because they do not study it. Others, though, refuse to believe authentic Catholic teachings, especially those of the fifth and sixth commandments. C. S. Lewis stated the problem in his book, *Screwtape Letters*, when he spoke about those refusing to believe in faith. He said (He was speaking for the devil!) "…a moderated religion is as good for us [devils] as no religion at all—and more amusing."[12] We may moderate our drinking habits or our food intake or our speed on the highways, but there is never a moderation to faith. We either follow Jesus or we don't.

The Catholic Church is the foundation of truth. The *Catechism of the Catholic Church* says, "'Outside the Church there is no salvation'" and "This affirmation is not aimed at those who, through no fault of their own, do not know Christ and his Church…"[13] The following are the marks of the Catholic Church:

* **One**: One person, Jesus Christ, who unified humanity with one truth, founded it. He is truth and we unite ourselves to this truth.

* **Holy**: Christ was holy; therefore, the Church is holy.

* **Catholic** (or universal): The *Catechism of the Catholic Church* teaches, "First, the Church is catholic because Christ is present in her…." Second, "The Church is catholic because she has been sent out by Christ on a mission to the whole of the human race [to proclaim the Good News]…" (cf. Matthew 28:19).[14]

* **Apostolic**: Jesus died on the cross for the redemption of the world. He rose from the dead, ascended into heaven, and sent upon the Church the Holy Spirit, who descended on the Apostles at Pentecost. Christ, himself, chose the Apostles and sent them on a mission. The faith that they professed is kept and handed on. The *Catechism of the Catholic Church* says the Church "continues to be taught, sanctified, and guided by the Apostles until Christ's return, through their successors in pastoral office…."[15] (cf. Matthew 28:16-20, Acts 1:8, 1 Corinthians 9:1, 15:7-8, Galatians 1:1, Acts 2:42).

Again, the Church is one; it does not differ in its beliefs. It is holy; it does not try to change God's laws. It is catholic (universal); it does not follow psychic "New Age" thinking. It is apostolic; it follows Christ and his Apostles and there is no other God before it. We must not turn "justice into poison…" (Amos 6:12). How can you tell your children they must compassionately discern the difference between the Catholic Church and other Christian groups (churches)?

_____

_____

_____

_____

Read what scripture says about false teaching. You are either "justified" or "condemned" (Matthew 12:37) on the grounds of what you say. One false idea is that we are irrational if we try to change another person for the better and away from his sinfulness. If that were accurate, then Jesus would have had a neurosis. The truth is, we try to change ourselves first. Then, balanced in our faith, we seek perfection of the Holy Spirit and we must reveal our beliefs. We must, however, spread the truth in a loving manner and avoid hiding our faith. It would be a sin of omission not to spread truth. Spreading the truth of Christ brings love and peace to our soul and perhaps persecution to the person. Christ was persecuted for his teachings. As we learned in Chapter III, though, he triumphed on the last day. Compose a prayer and ask the wisdom of the Holy Spirit to acquaint your family and friends with the truth and beauty of the Church. Share it with your children.

_____
_____
_____
_____
_____

Christ wants us to "'preach the gospel to the whole creation. He who believes and is baptized will be saved....'" (Mark 16:15-16). He wants us to stand against evil. You are not being judgmental; you are saving victims from being deceived as illustrated in Exercises 30 and 31 like Jesus did.

74. Put our faith to work

We grow closer to Christ when we recognize him in others, and come to the assistance of those in need. In reality, there may be problems in your own home, and you may need help such as in the following: divorce_____, alcoholism_____, neglect_____, abandonment_____, abuse_____, incest_____, death_____, poor health_____, poverty_____, loneliness_____, joblessness_____, other_____. Determine if your priest or others in your church community have help available for you in these areas if you need them. Other help is listed in the community services section in your telephone directory. Still other sources are schools, psychologists, and physicians listed in the yellow pages. Then too, a family member or close friend may be your best source of consolation.

Perhaps this is the time you can earnestly and prayerfully address dysfunction in your family if there is some. Many times, dysfunction is caused by no fault of our own. If it was from a shortcoming, however, (and if you feel comfortable about it) express to your family your sorrow and firm will to make it better, so that this does not pass on from generation to generation as it may have in the past.

_____

_____

_____

_____

Whether or not the above concerns exist in your household, young people can develop an awareness of divorce, dysfunctional households, and so forth in their communities, and at least talk about problem solving. If they verbally practice problem solving, they can more readily prevent these concerns in their own future. They can also develop awareness for the volunteer community needs by speaking out and reaching out to others. Ask your young adult questions such as the following:

(a) What do you think causes (<u>example: divorce</u>)?

(b) How do you think people could prevent (<u>example: divorce</u>)?

(c) How could you help someone in this situation? (Use the Corporal and Spiritual Works of Mercy in the back of the book.)

(d) How could your Christian community help someone in this situation?

(e) Where else could one go for help?

Compose a short prayer of thanksgiving for the blessings you have, and say it in unison with your family.

_____

_____

_____

_____

At times, parents and families need extra encouragement. St. Joseph's Covenant Keepers gives weekend seminars throughout the country for men; Catholic Resources Center, sponsored by St. Joseph Communications gives Catholic family conferences; and The Christian Mother organization has monthly meetings in most areas for women. Catholic Familyland provides entertainment, fun, and learning. Fatima Family Apostolate forms small prayer groups. Find these and others in the bibliography at the end of this chapter.

Respect Other Faiths

In our mobile society, children meet and make friends with people of many different faiths. Jesus asks that we love our neighbors, but he does not mean we should believe everything they believe. Children get confused, even adults get confused sometimes. Do we shut out those preaching door-to-door? No, of course not. Should we kindly say "no thanks?" Maybe, if we think we can't answer their questions. Should we tell them about our faith? Yes, if we are strong in our faith. Other Christians and non-Christians love God or deity, too. They have temples, churches, synagogues, mosques, and so forth for worship. We respect other faiths, but we do not agree with all their varying beliefs. The following facts about the Protestant Christian faith and non-Christian faiths will help your children know what to say if they are confronted.

75. Other Christians

Protestantism began with the Reformation in 16th Century Europe. They base their faith and worship from that time. Although there were five divisions in the beginning, there are hundreds of denominations now. According to the 1999 Catholic Almanac, "The majority of U.S. Protestants belong to the following denominations: Baptist, Methodist, Lutheran, Presbyterian, Protestant Episcopal, the United States Church of Christ, the Christian Church (Disciples of Christ), Evangelicals."[16] John S. Hardon, S.J. said, they believe fairly consistently, (a) the Bible, not Church authority or Sacred Tradition, is "the only rule of faith…" (b) justification comes from "faith alone, excluding supernatural merit and good works…" (c) "the universal priesthood of believers, excluding a distinct…priesthood [is] divinely empowered through ordination to teach, govern, and sanctify the people of God."[17] These, of course, are not Catholic beliefs.

Protestant reformers disagreed with certain elements, such as secularism, superstition, unfit clergy, and corruption, in the Catholic Church. There was good reason to question some bad aspects in Church religious and laity. Nevertheless, looking back in history, the Apostles would never have left Jesus because of Judas. There will always be a "Judas" in Catholic *and* Protestant Churches, since all have sinned. Just as we make a good confession (from mortal sin) before we take communion, we must all repent before we can become one with our brothers and sisters. Christian faiths must strive for the same truth. Blessed John the XXIII asked us to "seek what unites, not what divides." Catholic and Protestant churches have much in common: the Bible, God, Jesus, Baptism, Commandments, and so forth. Commonality, though, doesn't mean that

Catholics should ignore our beliefs. It means that we should proclaim our Catholic goodness and strive to be one in truth, not one in compromise.

How would you tell your children about our difference and likeness with other Christian faiths? How would you tell children about our hope and prayer of all again being one faith? (Find help with the Bible, justification, and authority from Exercises 71 to 73 of this chapter.)

_____

_____

_____

_____

76. Non-Christians

Non-Christian Churches are quite different from each other. Some characteristics of a few of them follow:

Judaism: According to the Catholic Almanac, "Judaism is a religion of the Hebrew Bible…[It] was identified with the Israelites, and achieved distinctive form and character as the religion of the *Torah*…" In some contexts it is the first five books of the Old Testament: Genesis, Exodus, Leviticus, Numbers, and Deuteronomy. They believe in God, the prophets, Sabbath, coming of God's kingdom and final judgment.[18]

Islam: Islam originated from Muhammad who was believed to be "…God's last and greatest prophet." They believe: "There must be no murmurings at His [the Creator's] decrees; life must be placed in His hands, in trust and love. The *fatalism* which has come to be regarded as part of the Moslem creed had no place in the system established by Mohammed, who again and again repudiated the idea. Mohammed taught reform, not revolution."[19]

Hinduism and Buddhism: The Catholic Almanac says, "Hinduism and Buddhism—along with Confucianism, Taoism, Shinto, Native American Traditions and other religions—unlike Judaism, Christianity, and Islam, are called non-Abrahamic because in them Abraham is not shared as a father in faith."[20]

Hinduism: Hinduism originated in India "by Aryan tribes, originally from the present southern U.S.S.R.…around 1500 B.C." Their first great god is Brahma, but they "recognize approximately 330,000,000 gods." They believe the soul is sacred, "all living organisms, including insects, have souls….the cow is considered most sacred."[21]

Buddhism: "The Buddha was a great religious teacher who lived about five centuries before Christ. He was born in southern Nepal, though most of his work was done in north India." They direct their thoughts to the "good and true." They control their emotions and refuse "to do anything wrong." "Any man who is ready and able to do all of this can discover for himself the final and perfect happiness."[22]

As you can see, non-Christian religions have some positive attributes, but we, as Roman Catholics, have many differences with them, too. Explain this to your children. Explain that we believe Jesus was both God and man. He was Redeemer, Crucified, Son of God, Beloved, Almighty, Creator, Sanctifier. He is our Lord and Savior Jesus Christ. He gave Peter "the keys of the kingdom of heaven" (Matthew 16:19). This is why we do not believe in the prophets only. This is why we do not believe in Muhammad or Buddha. This is why we do not believe in "only" the Bible. The Church formulated it about 300 years *after* Jesus lived on Earth. We lived by the tradition of Jesus during those 300 years, as we do now. In other words, the first Christians followed Jesus (and the authority given by him to Peter and to the line of popes after that) as Catholics will do until the end of time. Relate this and other reasons why you follow Jesus, authority, Catholic tradition, *and* the Bible. Review this and other articles of faith, such as sacraments and the Mass, in Exercises 71 to 73.

_____

_____

_____

_____

Children love to hear stories of your childhood. Are there faith stories you want to share with them? Who convinced you of your faith? Was it a kindly nun, a priest, your parents, a friend? What incident in your life of faith made you want to be a Catholic? Was it truth, love, and the true presence of Christ in the Eucharist? Share this with your children.

_____

_____

_____

_____

Identify Cults

While some cults formed in this century, some date back to the years before Christ and some practice pagan rituals. Cults are groups of followers devoted to an extreme or delusive cause. The book, *Cults, Sects, and the New Age*, by Rev. James J. LeBar says some are "pseudo-religious" cults, and others are "the therapy cults, the political cults, and even the business cults."[23] The dominating leaders, "false prophets" (Matthew 7:15), would not want you to know about deceitful practices described below. Neither would they want you to know the measures you can take to prevent your children from becoming involved.

77. Cults and SCARE

No one would tell you he was a cultist; you would have to figure it out yourself. One way to describe a cult to your children is to talk about the SCARE acronym described in Exercise 25. The oftentimes-charismatic leader or movement controls others with SCARE tactics, but with one insidious twist: They slowly induce you into their way of thinking, making you distrustful of the outside world. Some organize into groups because they believe in dangerous ideas such as suicide, abortion, militant politics, fraud, or tax evasion. Others have a hidden agenda so that they easily gain power and control over members. Let us further examine how cults or other sects sometimes operate.

Cult recruitment may develop in a way such as this, starting with fellowship and ending with control: Mark, the recruiter, meets Scott, the unsuspecting lonely person, in a library or discotheque, perhaps. Mark invites Scott to a meeting for what may or may not seem to be a good saving-the-world cause, such as protecting young children, cleaning up the environment, learning about religion, dispelling another race, evading taxes, and the like. Scott accepts, and finds a host of new friends. The charismatic leader of the group welcomes him and preaches truths jumbled with lies and sarcasm well into the night. Scott's tired mind cannot distinguish facts from fiction. Although the charismatic leader might preach repugnant ideas much of the time, he asks Scott to be staunchly positive and not negative. The leader discourages contrary thoughts and questions about the group. Scott feels guilty for having contradictory thoughts, but he feels attached to his new friends, so he keeps coming back, night after night. The group of "friends" makes more decisions for Scott, especially about his time, money, family, and acquaintances. Eventually, they eat, live, and work together. Finally, if Scott wants to leave, they scorn him and threaten him with spiritual and physical harm. Totally cut off from his original friends, family, job, and school, Scott only has friends in the cult. Leaving is difficult because he lost his ability to make decisions. He not only loses his contact with the outside world, but he is infiltrated with a pessimistic view of it. The outside world seems like an unfriendly, depressive, distrustful bleakness. Add to this difficulty, Scott may have no money, shelter, credit, or insurance. The story continues—the cult hooked Scott.

You might want to warn older children about cults. Read this story with them. For practice, together fill in the blank lines below to fit the SCARE tactics that correspond with ideas above.

<u>Secrecy</u>—from outside information and from loved ones

_____

_____

_____

<u>Control</u>—of mind, body, and spirit

_____

_____

<u>Addiction</u>—to money, fundraising, and the cult

_____

_____

<u>Ridicule</u>—for saving doubts and wanting to leave the group

_____

_____

<u>Excuses and Enemies</u>—laced with sarcasm and lies

_____

_____

_____

How can you help your children distinguish the difference between the gradual brainwashing from a cult leader as described, and from ordinary, everyday peer pressures from acquaintances? (For extra help, read Matthew 7:15-28 from the Bible.)

_____

_____

_____

Refer to Exercise 26 and discuss ways to resist peer pressure SCARE tactics of cults.

_____

_____

_____

_____

Please note that all cults do not operate in exactly the same way, but all have a destructive pattern.

78. Examine cults

Now, examine a few cult and/or sect facts as opposed to God's truth.

Witchcraft

The facts include:

* Using power, control, irresistible effect, appeal, magic, or seductiveness in their rituals.

* Giving false information, even if only a small percent of the time—their scheme is to give some good information, and then intermingle evil ideas.

* Idolizing the gods of nature: Reverend James J. LeBar describes a link between witchcraft and the New Age movement. He said, "Some witchcraft is associated with satanism, but it is more properly a pantheism worship of nature."[24]

The truth about God's way in opposition to witchcraft includes:

* Praying to God and having "a pure heart and a good conscience and sincere faith" (I Timothy 1:5).

* Understanding the first commandment, "'You shall not make for yourself a graven image...'" (Exodus 20:4).

* Reading the Gospel, "'There shall not be...divination...soothsayer...sorcerer...charmer...medium...wizard...'" (Deuteronomy 18:10-11).

* Reading the Old Testament, "And the Lord sent a plague upon the people, because they made the calf which Aaron made." (Exodus 32:35).

Satanism

The facts include some or all of the following:

* Following the Satanic Bible and one's own conscience instead of listening to God. Johnnette S. Benkovic in her book, *The New Age Counterfeit* said, "Ironically, even as public belief in him [devil] diminishes, cults and covens who worship Satan bloom and grow."[25]

* Nullifying good for evil as Reverend Lebar states, "It is the negation of everything positive and good, and the embodiment of all that is evil."[26]

* Recruiting members and claiming an opposing relationship to Jesus and Christianity.

* Using symbols such as the five-pointed star, swastika, upside-down-Star of David, and upside-down-cross on silver jewelry and black clothing.

* Practicing child, animal, sexual, or drug abuse, and vandalizing cemeteries or other community property.

* Belonging to one of at least three different types: Some are involved with the First Church of Satan, others are into ritual and criminal activities, and still others commit less serious crimes. None fit all above stereotypes.

   The truth about God's way in opposition to Satanism includes:

* Praising and obeying Christ, respecting life, and recognizing the devil exists. (cf. Acts 13:8-12.)

* Hearing the words of Jesus, "…'You shall not tempt the Lord your God'" (Matthew 4:7).

New Age

The facts of this "leaderless" movement may include all or some of the following:

* Preoccupying oneself with the philosophy, "Everything is God; and God is everything." Hence, there are "no standards of right and wrong.…" as stated in a Columbia Magazine feature by Russell and Marjorie Chandler, "The Magnet of New Age Mysticism."[27]

* Practicing mythical ideology and communication from beyond, as the Chandlers said: "What once was considered paranormal is now unwittingly

accepted as normal. Business seminars, nutrition classes, music tapes, TV shows, exercise routines, crystals and holistic therapies may thinly veil—or openly promote psychic beliefs."[28] They look for a higher dimension other than God.

* "...[M]oving contemporary man away from the Judeo-Christian perspective of the world to a monistic [interdependent] idealism," Johnnette S. Benkovic reveals.[29] Their use of words, such as enlightenment, new perspective, limitless potential, higher conscience, visualization, and personal transformation are clues to their dependence on self and the world rather than on God. Sometimes they deceive by injecting Bible, angels, and church into their ideology.

* Worshipping nature and channeling—Fr. Andrew Miles, OSB, writes about "The New Age Movement and Christianity." He said:

> More and more we hear of such things as channeling and astral projection, crystals and pendulums, ascended masters, past lives, and higher consciousness...
>
> ...They are often more involved with ecology than many Christians. It is still, however, essential to distinguish the creature from the Creator, lest we fall into the worship of nature and of the forces of nature—which is paganism....

He reported, it may lead people into "witchcraft."[30]

* Knowing that New Agers have a difficult time distinguishing good from evil, prayer from mantra, and heaven from earth.

The truth about God's way in opposition to the New Age Movement includes:

* Reading the Bible and knowing we are not God: 'Jesus said..."I am the way, the truth, and the life; no one comes to the Father but by me"' (John 14:6). John the Baptist realized he was, "'...not worthy to untie [the sandals on his feet]'" (Acts 13:25).

* Caring for nature but not worshipping it. Instead, we worship God (cf. Genesis 2:15).

* Reading the Psalms: "Thou hatest those who pay regard to vain idols..." (Psalm 31:6) and "Blessed is the man who makes the Lord his trust..." (Psalm 40:4).

* Recognizing we are Christian, we do not have divine powers, we can and do sin; and realizing death is final, and we do not come back, "men...die once, and after that comes judgment" (Hebrews 9:27).

* Knowing the New Age mysticism is "rooted in ancient spiritualities: Buddhism, Hinduism, Taoism, Zen, and Gnosticism."[31] (Hindus "find" themselves in yoga.)

* Recognizing the true Christian faith and the true Lord Jesus Christ as our Redeemer.

If you have children that experienced any items above on diverse groups, circle those areas and talk to them. Also, tell them that the New Age may be prevalent in many meetings they will attend. The New Age movement tells you to be positive. Being positive is good, sometimes; however, positive philosophy isn't always reasonable when we, for instance: fight secular sex education, halt a corrupt official, or stand against an abortion doctor. Thus, standing up for your faith and against sin can get tough, negative, or trying (at best). New Agers, on the other hand, who believe life on Earth is perfect, may very well have a sluggish response to evil or ignore it altogether and lose faith.

Have there been instances when cult-like groups tried to gain a stronghold in your state, your community, or even your church?_____ Would you feel comfortable sharing this with your children?_____ If so, how could you express this to them?

_____

_____

_____

_____

79. Prevention

"He who rides a tiger is afraid to dismount."—Ancient Chinese proverb. Those who choose diverse ideas and groups (in Exercises 77 and 78) have reason to be fearful of knowledgeable people. Choose to make your precious children knowledgeable, confident, and free from daring demons. Children need our unconditional love and attention to ward off the evils of cults.

The following ideas can help:

* Be informed about your children's lives. Is there a preoccupation with any of the following: drugs; horror movies; pornography; fantasy; magic; backward writing; black furnishings and clothing; crystal; games, such as, Dungeons and Dragons,

and Ouija boards; self-mutilation and death; secretive behavior; depression; or negative, hurtful actions?

* One survey said adults who joined cults never heard ghost stories as children. Evidence points there is a benefit to scary stories told on a Halloween eve. Then again, some Bible verses might make better "ghost stories." (See "Jonah and the Whale," Jonah 1:1 to 4:11; "The Earthquake," Acts 16:25-34; and "Noah's Ark," Genesis 6:5 to 8:22.)

* Face other warning signs and converse in reassuring ways. For instance, your children may spend much time in a New Age bookstore (most likely, it has a deceiving name). More severely, though, your children could find enticement in a cult of revengeful supremacists. In the first instance, your children may be simply curious. Teach them how to use libraries and Christian or Catholic bookstores to their advantage. In the second instance, if they are involved in an avenging situation, direct them to support systems in church and community. Tell them if someone promises them something that seems too good to be true, it probably is.

* Read library books that your children read. Most children's books are innocent and fun, but a few are degrading and dangerous. One book makes grandmothers appear rude and vulgar. Another turns mothers into witches. Still, another degrades Christianity, upholds magic, and makes witches and wizards of the occult virtuous while parents appear as abusive demons. These books have little or no value; explain to children the moral of it, if there is one, and then demonstrate why you do or do not like the book. Better yet, don't expose bad literature to them in the first place.

* Find out if cult activity is in your area.

* Remind children that you are always willing to talk anytime they are depressed or frightened.

* Review especially Exercises 1 and 2 and 7 to 11 on "God's Love" and "Work, Determination, and Goals." Young people mixed up with cults often have a rock-bottom opinion of themselves. Therefore, help children develop confidence by knowing God, by working at jobs, and by helping themselves and others. Confidence in the Lord, in one's future, and in the future of others is the avenue in which we develop one's character.

* Pray and have faith. Part of the "Spiritual Warfare Prayer" reads as follows:

> In the Holy Name of Jesus, I break and dissolve any and all curses, hexes, spells, snares, traps, lies, obstacles, deceptions, diversions...evil wishes, evil desires, hereditary seals, known and unknown, and every

dysfunction and disease from any source including my mistakes and sins...[32]

To order a copy of this prayer, check the bibliography.

* As stated earlier, a child who belongs to a cult finds it extremely difficult to leave. Seek professional help through the following: the Church (refer to Acts 16:16-18), law enforcement, school counselors, psychiatrists, psychologists, treatment clinics, and medical and state institutions. Another, Reverend James J. LeBar, can assist you in the bibliography.

Isolated and lonely young adults may attach themselves to anyone they find. Cults may be one of these dismal choices. Therefore, children need observation, direction, communication, prayer, and if necessary outside help.

Teach children about heavenly treasures. The Bible says, "Do not lay up for yourselves treasures on earth, where moth and rust consume and where thieves break in and steal, but lay up for yourselves treasures in heaven, where neither moth nor rust consumes and where thieves do not break in and steal. For where your treasure is, there will your heart be also" (Matthew 6:19-21). When young people know the difference between truth and myths, they become staunch defenders of truth in the Church, as priests, moms and dads, and single people spreading the word. How would you discuss the listings above? Discuss, also, how treasure rests in the shelter of discipline and faith, and how you plan to pass treasures onto future generations.

_____

_____

_____

_____

To walk in God's Kingdom and be happy with him forever, we must have discipline to turn away from "immorality, impurity, licentiousness, idolatry, sorcery, enmity, strife, jealousy, anger, selfishness, dissension, party spirit, envy, drunkenness, carousing, and the like...." (Galatians 5: 19-21). We must have a dawn of new faith, and we must believe in him, and help others know about sharing God's love and happiness in his Kingdom for Eternity. In short, we need the fruits of the Holy Spirit, "love, joy, peace, patience, kindness, goodness, faithfulness, gentleness, self-control..." (Galatians 5:22-23). It is not how we bend the rules so God serves us. It is how we follow the path of goodness so that we serve God and our fellow man. Paul and Barnabas "shook...the dust from their feet..." (Acts 13:51).

Dear Lord, we are temples of the Holy Spirit. Our souls belong to you. We will not disappoint you.

Final Letter to Parents

Congratulations, you laid the foundation of your children's morality in Chapters I, II, and III. You built the walls of facts in Chapters IV, V, and VI. You topped it with the roof of expectations through the discipline of faith in Chapter VII, and you sealed it to a respect for life and love with "Christ Jesus himself being the corner stone," (Ephesians 2:20). You and your children can be most thankful.

This is the age of exploding information. Most is good. Some is bad. Your children need to know how to select the best. Now, with your love and your guidance from Church sources and common facts, children can discern the difference between good and evil. This, however, is not the ending. This is the beginning. You might review sections of this book again, or teach from the *Catechism of the Catholic Church*. (Hint: Begin with the "In Brief" notes after each section of the Catechism, or by finding a topic of interest in its index.) A copy should be in every home. Excellent books, magazines, and tapes in the Resource pages of this book also keep the entire family up-to-date on life, faith, and good works.

We don't have to have kids who make poor choices about sexuality, drugs, and alcohol. We don't have to have kids who fall for the New Age jargon and stay away from the Church. We *can* have kids who make good decisions about life.

You will know when your children are ready to face peer pressure and say "no" to death and "yes" to life: (1) You will know when your children understand sacred life and follow the Word of God. (2) You will know when they have concern and respect for friends and family. (3) And, you will know when they want to serve God in this world and the next. Staying on God's team takes a lifetime of perseverance, prayer, and practice—and it begins with the grace of God and short five-minute increments of a parent's time.

One final prayer: Lord, I shall be as a shiny doorknob and uphold the Roman Catholic faith. I shall be a circle of friendship to my family. I shall hold the key to their future and shut out evil. I shall open it to our Lord's sunshine, and keep it in good working order—all in your name. "Thou dost keep him in perfect peace, whose mind is stayed on thee, because he trusts in thee" (Isaiah 26:3). Amen and may God bless, and may you love those children.

Mary Lee Dey

Endnotes:

1. *Catechism of the Catholic Church* (Washington, D.C.: United States Catholic Conference, 1997), Publication no. 5-110, #2228, p. 538.

2. Scott and Kimberly Hahn, *Rome Sweet Home Our Journey To Catholicism* (San Francisco: Ignatius Press, 1993), p. 172-173.

3. *Catechism of the Catholic Church*, op. cit., #2042-43, p. 493-94.

4. *Ibid.*, #2041, p. 493.

5. *Pillar of Fire Pillar of Truth* (San Diego: Catholic Answers, 1997), p. 29.

6. Steve Wood, *Wednesday Afternoon: Two Ways to Supercharge Your Marriage,* CF192 (P) Cassette tape, GRACE On Site (1996).

7. "*Prison Statistics,*" U.S. Department of Justice, Bureau of Justice Statistics (December 2002) Web site: www.ojp.usdoj.gov: p. 1.

8. *Catechism of the Catholic Church*, op. cit., #1030-1032, p. 268-269.

9. David Currie, *Born Fundamentalist* (San Francisco: Ignatius Press, 1996), p. 64.

10. Rev. Robert J. Fox, *The Catholic Faith* (Indiana: Our Sunday Visitor, Inc., 1986), p. 175.

11. Karl Keating, "How to Fight the Lies, Myths, and Half-Truths about Catholicism That Are Keeping Good People Out of the Catholic Church!" newsletter, Catholic Answers [San Diego] (1997), p. 2.

12. C.S. Lewis, *Screwtape Letters* (West Chicago: Lord and King Associates Publications, 1976), p 55.

13. *Catechism of the Catholic Church*, op. cit., #846, #847, p. 224.

14. Ibid., #830-#831, p. 220.

15. Ibid., #857, p. 227.

16. *1999 Catholic Almanac* (Huntington, IN: Our Sunday Visitor: 1999), p. 321.

17. John S. Hardon, S.J., *Pocket Catholic Dictionary* (New York: Image, 1985), p. 351.

18. *1999 Catholic Almanac*, op. cit., p. 325.

19. Walter Dill Scott, B.A., Ph.D., LL.D., Chairman of the Editorial Board, and Franklin J. Meine, PH. B. M.A., Editor-in-Chief, *The American Peoples Encyclopedia* (Chicago: The Spencer Press, Inc. 1948), p. 13-867, 69.

20. *1999 Catholic Almanac*, op. cit., p. 330.

21. William Benton Publisher, *Britannica Junior Encyclopedia* (U.S.A.: Plempton Press, 1968), p. 7-H-142-143.

22. Ibid., p. 385, 386.

23. Rev. James J. LeBar, *Cults, Sects, and the New Age* (Huntington, IN: Our Sunday Visitor Publishing Division, 1989), p. 17.

24. Ibid., p. 133.

25. Johnnette S. Benkovic, *The New Age Counterfeit* (Goleta, CA: Queenship Publishing, 1993), p. 89.

26. Lebar, op. cit., p. 130.

27. Russell Chandler and Marjorie Lee Chandler, "The Magnet of New Age Mysticism" *Columbia* (July 1990): p. 6.

28. Ibid.

29. Benkovic, op. cit., p. 4.

30. Fr. Andrew Miles, OSB, "The New Age Movement and Christianity" leaflet #71, (Pecos, New Mexico 87552: Dove Publications, n.d.).

31. Chandler, loc. cit.

32. "Spiritual Warfare Prayer" (Scottsdale, AZ 85252-1982: M.A.R.Y. Ministries).

Bibliography:

Arnold, Matthew. *Harry Potter, Delightful Diversion or Dangerous Deception.* Tehachapi, CA 93581: St. Joseph Communications, P.O. Box 1911 Suite 83, Telephone: with credit card 1-800-526-2151, 1-661-822-2050 (in CA), Web site: www.saintjoe.com, 2001.

Atkins, James. *Mass Confusion.* San Diego, CA 92177: Catholic Answers, P.O. Box 17490, Telephone: 1-888-291-8000, 1998.

Benkovic, Johnnette S. *The New Age Counterfeit.* Santa Barbara, CA: Queenship Publishing, 1993.

Budnik, Mary Ann. *Raise Happy Children Series, Looking for peace? Try Confession!* and other books. Springfield, IL 62704: R.B. Media, Inc., 154 Doral, Telephone: 1-217-546-5261, Fax: 217-546-0558, Web site: www.rbmediainc.com, 2000.

Catechism of the Catholic Church, publication no. 5-110. Washington, D.C.: United States Catholic Conference, 1997.

Catholic Exchange, your faith, your life, your world, gives daily readings, today's saint, and more. Web site: www.catholicexchange.com/.

Catholic Familyland, order *Its Purpose & Mission,* #188-796VK, provides entertainment, fun, and learning. Bloomingdale, Ohio 43910-7903: Catholic Familyland, 3375 County Road 36, Telephone: 1-800-FOR-MARY or 1-740-765-4301, Web site: www.familyland.org.

Catholic Resource Center, Catholic family conferences. West Covina, CA 91793: Saint Joseph Communications, inc., Telephone 1-813-868-3549, Web site: catholicresourcecenter.org.

Catholic World Report, magazine of the Christian tradition. San Francisco, CA 94159-1300: Catholic World Report, P.O. Box 591300, Telephone: (new orders) 1-800-651-1531, Web site: www.ignatius.com.

Christian Mothers, National Office of the Archconfraternity, organization has monthly meetings in most areas for women. Pittsburgh, PA. 15201-9990: Christian Mothers, 220-37th Street, Telephone: 1-412-683-2400.

Currie, David. *Born Fundamentalist.* San Francisco: Ignatius Press, 1996.

Divine Mercy Message and Devotion, booklet, prayers from diary of Saint Maria Faustina. Stockbridge, MA 01263: Marian Press, Marians of the Immaculate Conception, Telephone: 1-800-462-7426, Web site: www.marian.org, 1995.

Faith and Family, magazine for Catholic laity. Mt. Morris, IL 61045-0369: Faith and Family, P.O. Box 369, Telephone: 1-800-421-3230.

Faith and Life Series, for CCD programs, parents, schools, and home-schools. San Francisco: Ignatius Press, Telephone: 1-800-651-1531, Web site: www.ignatius.com, and www.CatecheticalResources.com.

Faith Facts, answers to questions on Catholic faith. Stuebenville, OH 43952: Emmaus Road Publishing, Telephone: 1-800-MY-FAITH or 1-740-283-2484, Web site: www.cuf.org, 1999.

FOCUS, Fellowship of Catholic University Students. Greeley, Colorado 80634: FOCUS, 4407 29th Street, Telephone 1-970-506-0751, Web site: www.focusonline.org.

Fox, Rev. Robert J. *Charter of the Fatima Family Apostolate,* how to form a small prayer-study group. Redfield, South Dakota 57469: Fatima Family Apostolate, P.O. Box 55, Fax: 1-605-472-4113, Telephone: (credit card) 1-800-213-5541, 1997.

Hahn, Scott, and Kimberly Hahn. *Rome Sweet Home Our Journey To Catholicism.* San Francisco: Ignatius Press, 1993.

Hayes, Rev. Edward J., et al. *Catholicism & Society.* Norwood, MA 02062: C. R. Publications Inc., 2003.

Keating, Karl. "Catholic Answers" newsletter, they also answer questions on a broad range of information about Scripture and Church teachings. San Diego 92177: Catholic Answers, P.O. Box 17490, Telephone: 1-619-541-1131, Web site: www.catholic.com.

Keating, Karl. *What Catholics Really Believe.* San Francisco, CA: Ignatius Press, 1992.

Kellmeyer, Steve. *Bible Basics.* Steubenville, OH: Basilica Press, 2000.

Lay Witness, monthly magazine to support, defend, and advance the efforts of the teaching Church. Steubenville, OH: Catholics United for the Faith, Telephone: 1-740-283-2484, Web site: www.cuf.org.

LeBar, Rev. James J., *Cults, Sects, and the New Age.* IN: Our Sunday Visitor Publishing Division, 1989.

Librarian's Guide to Catholic Resources on the Internet, apologetics, art, home-school and prayer. Web site: http://lgcr.tripod.com/index.html.

Lovasik, Rev. Lawrence G. S.V.D. *What Catholics Believe,* simplified course in Christian Doctrine based on Baltimore Catechism, emphasizes Holy Eucharist and Penance. Rockford, Illinois, 61105: Tan Books and Publishers, Inc., Box 424, Telephone: 1-800-437-5876, Web site: www.tanbooks.com, 1977.

Madrid, Patrick. *Surprised by Truth 2.* Manchester, New Hampshire: Sophia Institute Press, 2000.

Madrid, Patrick and Toni Collins and Michael O'Brien. *There's Something About Harry,* Catholic Analysis on "Harry Potter," two cassettes. Granville, OH

43023: Surprised by Truth, P.O. Box 640, Telephone: 1-800-553-6869, Web site: www.surprisedbytruth.com, 2001.

Mary Foundation, free audio tapes on confession and more. Fairview Park, OH 44126-0101: Mary Foundation, P.O. Box 26101, Web site: www.catholicity.com.

New Oxford Review, magazine covers issues of concern to orthodox Catholics. Berkeley: New Oxford Review, Room 171, 1069 Kains Avenue.

Pillar of Fire Pillar of Truth. San Diego 92177: Catholic Answers, P.O. Box 17490, Telephone: 1-619-541-1131, Web site: www.catholic.com, 1997.

Ray, Steve. *Conversion Testimony*, audio tape #7225. Tehachapi, CA 93581: St. Joseph Communications, P.O. Box 1911 Ste. 83, Telephone: with credit card 1-800-526-2151, 1-661-822-2050 (in CA), Web site: www.saintjoe.com, n.d.

Raymond, Brother John. *Catholics on the Internet.* Rocklin, CA: Prima Publishing, 2001.

Religious Education, "Faith and Life" and "Image of God" series. San Francisco: Ignatius Press, Telephone: 1-800-651-1531, Web site: www.ignatius.com.

Rossini, Ellen. *100 Activities*, based on *The Catechism of the Catholic Church*, grades 1 to 8. San Francisco: Ignatius Press, 1996.

Saint Joseph's Covenant Keepers, gives weekend seminars throughout the country for men. Port Charlotte, FL 33949: Family Life Center International, P.O. Box 6060, Telephone: 1-941-764-7725, Fax: 1-941-743-5352, Web site: www.familylifecenter.net.

"Spiritual Warfare Prayer," send $1.00 and a #10 SASE. Scottsdale, AZ 85252-1982: M.A.R.Y. Ministries, P.O. Box 1982.

Staples, Tim. *Seven Needs, Seven Answers, Seven Sacraments*, help youth turn to Christ and his Church, four cassettes #7919. Tehachapi, CA 93581: St. Joseph Communications, P.O. Box 1911 Ste. 83, Telephone: with credit card 1-800-526-2151, 1-661-822-2050 (in CA), Web site: www.saintjoe.com, n.d.

Stravinskas, Peter M. J. *The Catholic Response.* Indiana: Our Sunday Visitor, 1985.

Suprenant, Leon J., and Philip C. L. Gray. *Faith Facts.* Steubenville, OH: Emmaus Rood Publishing, 1999.

This Rock, magazine. San Diego 92177: Catholic Answers, P.O. Box 17490, Telephone: 1-888-291-8000, Web site: www.catholic.com.

U.S. National Conference of Catholic Bishops. 3211 Fourth Street, N.E., Washington, DC 20017-1194, Telephone: 1-202-541-3070 Fax: 1-202-541-3054, Web site: www.usccb.org. Canadian Conference, Web site: www.cccb.ca.

Vatican. Web site: www.vatican.va.

Welters, Sister M. Andrine, O.S.B. *My Confession Book*. Rockford, Illinois, 61105: Tan Books and Publishers, Inc., Box 424, Telephone: 1-800-437-5876, Web site: www.tanbooks.com, 1997.

Young Writers Workshop. *Kids Explore America's Catholic Heritage*. Boston: Pauline Books and Media, Web site: www.pauline.org, 2002.

Prayers, Works of Mercy, Commandments, and Beatitudes

The Lord's Prayer

Our Father, Who art in heaven, hallowed be Thy name: Thy kingdom come; Thy will be done on earth as it is in heaven. Give us this day our daily bread; and forgive us our trespasses as we forgive those who trespass against us; and lead us not into temptation, but deliver us from evil. Amen.

The Hail Mary

Hail Mary, full of grace! The Lord is with thee; blessed art thou among women, and blessed is the fruit of thy womb, Jesus. Holy Mary, Mother of God, pray for us sinners, now and at the hour of our death. Amen.

Glory Be To the Father

Glory be to the Father, and to the Son, and to the Holy Spirit, as it was in the beginning, is now, and ever shall be, world without end. Amen.

The Apostles' Creed

I believe in God, the Father Almighty, Creator of heaven and earth; and in Jesus Christ, His only Son, our Lord; Who was conceived by the Holy Spirit, born of the Virgin Mary, suffered under Pontius Pilate, was crucified, died and was buried. He descended into hell; the third day He arose again from the dead; He ascended into heaven, sits at the right hand of God, the Father Almighty; from thence He shall come to judge the living and the dead. I believe in the Holy Spirit, the holy Catholic Church, the communion of saints, the forgiveness of sins, the resurrection of the body, and life everlasting. Amen.

The Act of Contrition

O my God, I am heartily sorry for having offended You, and I detest all my sins, because of Your just punishments, but most of all because they offend You, my God, Who art all-good and deserving of all my love. I firmly resolve, with the help of Your grace, to sin no more and to avoid the near occasions of sin. Amen.

Hail Holy Queen

Hail, holy Queen, Mother of mercy, our life, our sweetness, and our hope, to you do we cry, poor banished children of Eve; to you do we send up our sighs, mourning and weeping in this valley of tears. Turn then, most gracious advocate, your eyes of mercy toward us; and after this our exile, show unto us the blessed fruit of your womb, Jesus. O clement, O loving, O sweet Virgin Mary, Queen of the most holy Rosary, pray for us that we may be worthy of the promises of Christ.

Morning Offering

O Jesus, through the immaculate heart of Mary, I offer You my prayers, works, joys and sufferings of this day, for all the intentions of your Sacred Heart, in union with the holy sacrifice of the Mass throughout the world, in reparation for my sins, for the intentions of all our associates, and in particular for the intention recommended this month by the Holy Father.

Evening Prayer

Oh God, I thank You for all the blessings I have received today. Forgive me all my sins. I am sorry for them all because I have deceived Thee. Bless me through the night, so I may do better tomorrow. Bless Father and Mother and all those who I love so that they may be happy. Jesus, Mary, and Joseph pray for me always, especially at the hour of my death. Amen.

Grace Before Meals

Bless us, O Lord, and these Thy gifts, which we are about to receive from Thy bounty through Christ, our Lord. Amen.

Grace After Meals

We give Thee thanks, O Lord, for all Thy gifts, which we have received from Thy bounty through Christ, our Lord. Amen.

Angel of God

Angel of God, My Guardian Dear, to whom His love commits me here, ever this day be at my side, to light and guard, to rule and guide. Amen.

St. Michael Prayer

St. Michael the Archangel, defend us in battle. Be our protection against the wickedness and snares of the devil. May God rebuke him, we humbly pray, and do thou, O Prince of the Heavenly Host, by the Divine Power, thrust into Hell, Satan and all the evil spirits who roam through the world seeking the ruin of souls. Amen.

The Corporal Works of Mercy

1. Feed the hungry.
2. Give drink to the thirsty.
3. Clothe the naked.
4. Shelter the homeless.
5. Comfort the imprisoned.
6. Visit the sick.
7. Bury the dead.

The Spiritual Works of Mercy

1. Admonish sinners.
2. Instruct the uninformed.
3. Counsel the doubtful.
4. Comfort the sorrowful.
5. Be patient with those in error.
6. Forgive offenses.
7. Pray for the living and the dead.

The Ten Commandments

1. I am the Lord Thy God; thou shalt not have strange gods before Me.
2. Thou shalt not take the name of the Lord Thy God in vain.
3. Remember thou keep holy the Sabbath Day.
4. Honor thy father and thy mother.
5. Thou shalt not kill.
6. Thou shalt not commit adultery.
7. Thou shalt not steal.
8. Thou shalt not bear false witness against thy neighbor.
9. Thou shalt not covet thy neighbor's wife.
10. Thou shalt not covet thy neighbor's goods.

The Beatitudes

"Blessed are the poor in spirit, for theirs is the kingdom of heaven.
Blessed are the meek, for they shall possess the earth.
Blessed are they who mourn, for they shall be comforted.
Blessed are they who hunger and thirst for justice, for they shall be satisfied.
Blessed are the merciful, for they shall obtain mercy.
Blessed are the clean of heart, for they shall see God.
Blessed are the peacemakers, for they shall be called children of God.
Blessed are they who suffer persecution for justice' sake, for theirs is the kingdom of heaven."

Index

0-595-31922-X

Printed in the United States
39267LVS00004B/292-303